D1495025

TUCSON
TO
TOMBSTONE
A GUIDE TO SOUTHEASTERN ARIZONA

TEXT BY TOM DOLLAR

PHOTOGRAPHY BY
ARIZONA HIGHWAYS CONTRIBUTORS

ARIZONA HIGHWAYS
BOOKS

(FRONT COVER) *Snow frosts the Santa Catalina Mountains while Tucson basks in the warm desert below.* GILL C. KENNY
(INSIDE FRONT COVER) *Sunrise from Mount Graham illuminates the ridge lines of southeastern Arizona.* DAVID MUENCH
(ABOVE) *The lush grasslands of the San Rafael Valley epitomize southeastern Arizona's ranch country.* JACK DYKINGA

TUCSON TO TOMBSTONE

Winner of the 1996 Publishers Marketing Association Benjamin Franklin Award for Best Travel Guide and Narrative

Published by the Book Division of *Arizona Highways* magazine, a monthly publication of the Arizona Department of Transportation, 2039 West Lewis Avenue, Phoenix, AZ 85009.   Telephone: (602) 712-2200   Web site: www.arizonahighways.com
Win Holden — Publisher / Bob Albano — Managing Editor / Evelyn Howell and PK Perkin McMahon — Associate Editors / Peter Ensenberger — Photography Director / Mary Winkelman Velgos — Art Director / Kevin J. Kibsey — Design and Illustration / Cindy Mackey — Production Director
Still-life photography on pages 6, 29, 51, 64, and 84 by Carltons' Photographic.
Copyright © 1995 by the Department of Transportation, State of Arizona. Fourth edition, 2001 (fourth printing overall). All rights reserved. No part of this book may be reproduced in any form or by any means without permission of the publisher.
Printed in China
Library of Congress Number 94-080146   ISBN 0-916179-61-3

CONTENTS

INTRODUCTION

Basin and range. That's what geographers call the terrain in southeastern Arizona. Fault-block mountain ranges, shaped by cataclysmic upthrusting of enormous chunks of the Earth's crust, run across this portion of the

(OPPOSITE PAGE) *The setting sun burnishes saguaro cacti at the mouth of Pima Canyon in the Santa Catalina Mountains. The Catalinas, to the north of Tucson, provide a dramatic, scenic backdrop for the city.* JACK DYKINGA (ABOVE) *The Mount Lemmon Highway leads up a sky island.* INGE MARTIN

state. Steep and craggy on one side, and relatively gently sloping on the other, these mountains line up in an essentially northwest-southeast orientation. In between lie flat, sometimes quite broad, valleys, or basins. Thus, the splendidly succinct description: basin and range.

Physiographers divide Arizona's basin and range province into two parts: the Sonoran Desert section lying west of Tucson, and the Mexican Highland section to the east.

In the southeastern corner, the mountains become higher, more broad-backed, and spread out. These are southeastern Arizona's "sky islands," soaring higher than most other mountains in the state. Several peaks among the sky islands tower more than 9,000 feet. The tallest, Mount Graham in the

Pinaleno Mountains, tops out at 10,717 feet. East of Tucson, the intermontane valleys are broader, higher, wetter, and grassier than those to the west. Historically, some of the best cattle grazing in the region was in these valleys — Santa Cruz, San Rafael, San Pedro, Sulphur Springs, San Bernardino, and San Simon.

Calling out the names of these sky islands is a recitation of southeastern Arizona's cultural lineage: Huachuca, an Apache word meaning thunder; Rincon, Spanish for narrow valley or canyon; and Dragoon, the term referring to heavily armed, mounted U.S. Army troops who once were stationed in the area southeast of Tucson.

Those names and names of mountain ranges like Santa Catalina, Santa Rita,

Chiricahua, Galiuro, and Pinaleno reflect the linguistic imprint that Indian, Spanish, and Anglo-American people left on the land.

When I think of sky islands, I recall a midwinter drive I took to the summit of the Santa Catalinas soon after I arrived in Tucson years ago. The trip encapsulates for me the experience of living in southeastern Arizona's basin and range terrain.

I'd read extensively about the natural history of Arizona and was prepared, I thought, for what I would see. Still, what I recall most was my utter astonishment at the changing scenes as I climbed from the desert basin, elevation about 2,500 feet, up to Mount Lemmon's 9,157-foot summit.

Picture a sunny day in January with shirtsleeve weather at the base of the mountain. Only a few lamb's-wool clouds are pinned against a deep blue sky. For the first few miles on the Mount Lemmon Highway, the desert scenery does not change — saguaro cacti, prickly pear, ocotillo, cholla, and paloverde dominate the landscape. Then, as the road switchbacks up the mountain's lower portions, abundant grasses and the first few yucca plants appear. By the time I reach Molino Basin, elevation 4,500 feet, most of the desert plants have disappeared. Evergreen oaks dot the grassy terrain, and cottonwoods and willows grow on the margins of dry creek beds. Cool air bathes my bare arm resting on the frame of the open car window. I climb on.

Suddenly, the sun dodges out of sight, dark clouds boil across a deep canyon beside the road, and raindrops spatter on my windshield. I roll up the car windows, and through the streaks of rain on them I see manzanita bushes. The scrub-oak woodlands begin to give way to juniper and piñon trees.

At the Bear Canyon picnic ground, the first spar-like trunks of ponderosa pine loom beside the highway. In the canyon bottom, Arizona sycamore, ash, cypress, and walnut trees grow beside running water. A few wet snowflakes kiss the windshield. Old snow lies in deeper hollows in the

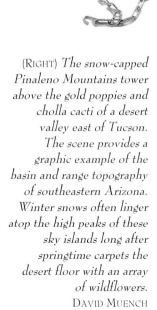

(RIGHT) *The snow-capped Pinaleno Mountains tower above the gold poppies and cholla cacti of a desert valley east of Tucson. The scene provides a graphic example of the basin and range topography of southeastern Arizona. Winter snows often linger atop the high peaks of these sky islands long after springtime carpets the desert floor with an array of wildflowers.*
DAVID MUENCH

6

spot a chair lift trundling toward the ski runs. A few skiers schuss down the slope, spraying powdery snow.

I step from my car into the crisp air. The temperature hovers at freezing, yet I'm comfortable in a heavy sweater as I walk around for a bit.

Back in the car, I turn around and drive down to Summerhaven, park, and trudge up the road through deepening snow toward Marshall Gulch. There, I leave the roadway and hike up the trail. Towering 300-year-old Douglas fir trees grow on the north slopes. After a short distance my progress is blocked by drifts too deep to cross without snowshoes. I retrace my steps.

Back at Summerhaven, I watch red-cheeked desert dwellers frolic in new snow. Gradually the chill seeps into my bones, so I duck into a cafe for a cup of hot cider before heading back down the mountain road to Tucson.

On that trip I had the uncanny feeling that I not only was climbing a mountain, but also passing from one country to another, and with each passage moving into different weather and species of plants and animals.

One of the books I had read described the experience as like driving from Mexico to Canada in a single afternoon. Much later, after a lot more reading and many explorations of other mountain ranges in southeastern Arizona, I began to make sense of what I had experienced on the first trip.

What I learned was that gaining 1,000 feet of elevation drops the temperature about 3.5 degrees Fahrenheit.

woods. A roadside sign warns of ice on the pavement, and another sign reads "Snowplow Ahead." By the time I reach Windy Point, elevation 6,600 feet, tire chains are necessary. After installing them, I walk across the road to a viewpoint, where on clear days the Tucson valley is visible. But on this day, snow swirls into dark canyons.

Slowed to a crawl now, and downshifted to my lowest gear, I inch up the mountain. I drive past Geology Vista, where in the weeks to come I'll scan the big mountain ranges to the east through binoculars. I creep across a narrow hogback ridge dropping off so steeply on both sides that my palms sweat. I'm losing heart, thinking of turning back. Then, amazingly, the clouds part, and I break into open sunshine.

I've passed through a high-altitude snow squall and come out the other side. The pine woods all around are full of snow, sparkling and fresh. On I drive, past a locked gate and sign: "Rose Canyon. Closed for Winter." Rounding a curve, I meet a snowplow with a line of cars trailing it as it cleaves a path down the mountain road.

Nearing the mountaintop village of Summerhaven, 26 miles up, I turn right and climb toward Ski Valley, the southernmost commercial ski slope in the United States. The bare trunks of quaking aspen trees resemble immense spear shafts hurled into snow drifts up the slopes from the road. A final turn and I

(OPPOSITE PAGE) *Summer ferns and columbines cover the forest floor beneath towering ponderosa pines in Marshall Gulch in the Santa Catalina Mountains less than an hour's drive from the desert city of Tucson.* JACK DYKINGA (ABOVE) *Snow frosts the craggy Catalina Mountains near San Pedro Point.* GEORGE WUERTHNER (BELOW) *Desert dwellers capture a snowman atop the Catalinas at Ski Valley, the southernmost ski area in the United States.* P.K. WEIS

Such a drop is roughly equivalent to moving 300 miles closer to the Arctic Circle. Thus, in driving up to Mount Lemmon I had gained nearly 7,000 feet and simulated in one hour the experience of traveling some 2,000 miles north of Tucson.

Higher not only means cooler, but also wetter. That's especially the case above 9,000 feet, where annual precipitation exceeds 35 inches. The weather acts as an invisible barrier, stopping plants dependent on cool, wet weather from migrating down, and desert plants from moving upward. Likewise, animals dependent on specific plants for food and shelter are more or less sequestered in the environmental niches of those plants. Abert's squirrel, for example, remains above 7,000 feet, where pine cones — its chief food supply — are plentiful. Biologists describe environmental niches linked to elevation as "life zones."

On my drive I started in the Lower Sonoran Life Zone and climbed into the Upper Sonoran Zone as I traveled beyond saguaro cacti into the grassy, oak woodlands.

Farther on, between 6,500 and 8,000 feet, I moved through a Transition Zone in which ponderosa pines grow. Nearing the top, above 8,000 feet, I entered the Canadian Life Zone with its aspens, Douglas fir, and boreal weather. Higher still, in the Hudsonian Life Zone, grow spruce-fir forests typical of northern Canada.

(BELOW) *A monument near Lochiel, on the Mexican border, honors Fray Marcos de Niza, who in 1539 crossed Arizona in search of the fabled Seven Cities of Gold.* RANDY A. PRENTICE (BOTTOM) *River rock and a weathered cross mark graves of early Spanish settlers in the cemetery at Tumacácori National Historic Park. The mission was built in 1802.* DAVID MUENCH

CONQUISTADORS AND PADRES CREATE A CULTURAL LEGACY

The first European to step onto Arizona soil probably was the Spaniard Alvar Nuñez Cabeza de Vaca. Stranded on the Texas coast after a shipwreck in 1528, he was captured by Indians. He and three companions escaped and over the next eight years made their way back to Mexico City on foot. It is likely that they crossed the southeastern tip of Arizona on the way.

His imagination undoubtedly kindled by Spanish legends about the Seven Cities of Cíbola and stories told by native Americans, Cabeza de Vaca spun wonderful tales about great riches somewhere north of his route.

Enthralled by the prospect of riches, the viceroy of Mexico, Antonio de Mendoza, ordered Fray Marcos de Niza, a Franciscan monk, to travel north and search out the Seven Cities. De Niza's guide was Esteban the Moor, who had been with Cabeza de Vaca on the trek from Texas to Mexico.

Traveling ahead of de Niza along the San Pedro River Valley in April 1539, Esteban erected crosses to guide those who were to follow.

Esteban reached one of the Zuni villages, but he was killed by the Indians. De Niza, far behind because he had stopped to provide ministering at Indian villages along the way, eventually arrived at what he believed to be the first and smallest of the Seven Cities. Hearing of Esteban's fate, de Niza was too fearful to enter the city.

Nevertheless, he returned to Mexico with tales of fabulous wealth. These stories prompted the first Spanish *entrada* — an entrance — into the region in February 1540.

Moving north from Mexico, Francisco Vásquez de Coronado led more than 225 mounted conquistadors; 62 foot soldiers; nearly 700 Indian wranglers, shepherds, and servants; and some 1,500 horses, mules, and other livestock. Moving along the route blazed by Esteban and Fray Marcos, the Coronado expedition passed through Arizona and into New Mexico, arriving at a Zuni village in July 1540. Quickly, Coronado conquered the pueblo and set

up a command post from which he sent out scouting parties.

The reports of fabulous wealth, Coronado soon discovered, were lies. There were six pueblos, not seven. Constructed of stone and humble, sun-baked bricks, none housed the promised opulence. Side expeditions proved equally futile — there was no gold or silver or precious gems, only Indians determined to defend their territory.

(A part of the trail that Coronado is believed to have forged through Arizona follows what now is U.S. Route 191 between the towns of Morenci and Eagar. The route is a part of the state's Parkway, Historic, and Scenic Road system.)

After exploring all the way to what now is Kansas, Coronado returned to Mexico City in disgrace. It was 40 years before the Spaniards attempted another entrada into Arizona.

Although priests often accompanied early Spanish explorers, it was not until the arrival of members of the Society of Jesus that real missionary work began in southeastern Arizona.

The black-robed Jesuits made their way north from Mexico City, using the desert river valleys as their highways.

Eusebio Francisco Kino, often called "the padre on horseback," came in 1691. Of all the Spanish explorers, clerical and secular, his legacy is the greatest.

Trained as a cartographer, he left carefully drawn maps showing the extent of his travels between 1691 and 1702. Kino's first mission was established at a Pima Indian village on a small plateau above the Santa Cruz River, not far from present-day Nogales.

The Indians living there called their village Guevavi. It was positioned on high ground in a long, narrow valley with river banks lined with tall cottonwood trees. Natural ramparts at the southern end of the plateau guarded its approach from the upstream side.

Kino believed that with a *cabecera*, a main church, a priest from this site could serve several *visitas*, or mission outposts.

Ten years later, in 1701, the mission Los Santos Angeles San Gabriel y San Rafael de Guevavi was established south of what now is Tucson, and Hispanic Arizona was born. ☙

(ABOVE LEFT) *The verdant valley along the San Pedro River has been a conduit for travelers for millennia —* *early hunter-gatherers, nomadic American Indians, Spanish conquistadors and missionaries, and railroad passengers riding between Benson and Naco.*
PETER KRESAN
(ABOVE) *Tom Dollar, who relishes the outdoors, is a frequent contributor to* Arizona Highways *magazine. He has written for* Audubon, Bicycle Guide, Wildlife Conservation, Modern Maturity, The New York Times, The Mother Earth News, *and other publications. He lives in southeastern Arizona, a region he describes as "a wonderland." This is his second book for* Arizona Highways. *His first was* Indian Country: A Guide to Northeastern Arizona. JACK DYKINGA

THE OLD PUEBLO

**CITY ON THE DESERT
DRAWS ITS IMAGE
WITH THE COLORS
OF THREE CULTURES**

Chapter 1

The setting is splendid. That's the first thing you notice as you stand atop Sentinel Peak looking east toward the city's center just across the usually dry Santa Cruz River. Along the river the Spaniards built an adobe presidio as a military base to protect the region from marauding Indians before there was a United States of America. Known locally as "A Mountain" for the big whitewashed letter "A" near its summit, Sentinel Peak is an ideal spot to survey the cityscape. From here, the city fans north and east across the valley toward the Santa Catalina and Rincon mountains, two of the ranges that shelter the Tucson basin.

Landmarks pop into view: the red-brick buildings and the immense stadium amphitheater of the University of Arizona, the carefully ruled landing strips of Davis-Monthan Air Force Base, the twin towers of St. Augustine Cathedral, and the glass-and-steel office buildings dominating the downtown skyline of this modern metropolis that sometimes is called the "Old Pueblo," a fond reference to the city's origins as an outpost of New Spain.

In the immediate foreground, Interstate 10 runs north to Phoenix and east to El Paso; a little south, Interstate 19 branches off and heads for the Mexican border at Nogales. Ten miles south of the city and just west of I-19, Mission San Xavier del Bac, the "White Dove of the Desert," shimmers under the sun.

Across the I-10 freeway, the low-slung buildings and green lawns of the Tucson Convention Center sprawl over several city blocks. The annual Gem and Mineral Show is in town. It's the biggest such show in the world, and the convention complex is swarming with activity.

You can't see it from here, but two

(OPPOSITE PAGE) Symbolizing Tucson's persona of a modern metropolis with Spanish roots reaching back more than 200 years, the bell towers of St. Augustine Cathedral contrast with the steel and glass of office buildings. TOM BEAN *(ABOVE) The Commissary Building is among the restored structures in the Fort Lowell Historic District.* RANDY A. PRENTICE

blocks south of the Convention Center, tucked into a niche in an adobe wall near the corner of Main and Simpson in an old neighborhood called Barrio El Hoyo, is El Tiradito, a wishing shrine put there in the 1870s. Many folk stories explain the origin of the shrine; all share the elements of mistaken identity and the tragic spilling of innocent blood.

One widely credited story tells of El Tiradito, "the little outcast or castaway." He was a young man who traveled from Sonora, Mexico, to visit a sister here in this barrio. The sister's husband, an older man unaware of this brother from Mexico, arrived home to find the two talking closely together. In a fit of jealous rage, he killed the young man with an ax. If you light a candle for the castaway soul of the innocent man killed here, it is believed that your wishes will come true.

To make way for the convention complex to the north, nine square blocks of Barrio Histórico were razed — homes, cafes, tradesmen's shops, stores, saloons, theaters — stripping the heart from Tucson's oldest and largest Mexican-style neighborhood. In 1971, when proposed freeway development threatened Barrio El Hoyo and El Tiradito itself, petitioners visited the shrine to light candles and pray for divine intercession. The community rallied to protect El Tiradito and the historic neighborhood. Eventually the bulldozers were stopped, freeway plans were abandoned, and a piece of Tucson's essentially Sonoran soul was saved.

Following the tradition of naming places after Roman Catholic saints, the Spanish pioneers, who in 1775 received orders to move their garrison 40 miles north from Tubac to a site along the Santa Cruz River, called it Presidio San Agustín del Tucson. The latter part of the name was borrowed from Pima Indians, who called their village on this spot *chuk-son*, meaning simply "place at the base of the dark mountain."

The presidio was moved here to protect settlers and travelers from Apache Indians. Thus, one year before there was a United States of America, Tucson became the northernmost Sonoran military outpost of New Spain. From the presidio, soldiers ranged as far north as the Tonto Basin, near Phoenix, and east to the San Francisco River, near what now is the border with New Mexico.

For 80 years — first under Spanish rule, then Mexican rule after 1822 — daily life in the Tucson garrison resembled that of rural Sonora.

Near the base of Sentinel Peak just west of the Santa Cruz River, Tucsonenses, as Tucson residents still call themselves, tapped clear springs to feed their *acequias*, the canal system that irrigated agricultural fields outside the walled presidio. They bathed, washed

Among the colorful threads of Hispanic traditions weaving through Tucson's cultural fabric is El Tiradito, a wishing shrine. Here the faithful light candles and offer prayers each evening. Legend holds that if the candles burn through the night then the prayers will be answered. Believers ask for a host of favors, ranging from cures for illness to good luck at hunting. Hispanics, Indians, and Anglos believe in the tradition of El Tiradito.
GILL C. KENNY

their clothes, and watered their livestock in the Santa Cruz River, a perennial stream until the early 20th century.

From thick river-bottom mesquite bosques, they gathered wood to heat their homes and fire their outdoor adobe ovens. Then at night, everyone left the fields to enter the presidio through a single massive gate, which was shut and bolted for security. The walls, extending 750 feet on four sides, enclosed slightly more than 12 acres of ground. Three feet thick at the bottom, they rose to a height of about 12 feet. Inside the walls were barracks for soldiers, an armory and powder magazine, a small church and cemetery, and a house for the commandant. Civilian houses were squat adobe huts built flush against the walls. From the roofs of the houses, soldiers could stand and shoot over the wall. The west wall ran alongside El Camino Real, which means "the royal highway." It extended all the way from Mexico City to this Sonoran outpost. Later, when Anglos arrived,

the street was renamed Calle Real, which means "the royal street," and later still, Main Avenue, its current name.

Pioneer Tucsonenses often felt that they were battling alone to hold the Apaches at bay. So forsaken did they feel, in fact, that in 1828, during the early period of Mexican rule, they threatened to abandon the presidio. The Gadsden Purchase of 1853 brought Tucson into the United States of America as part of the Territory of New Mexico. The winds of change were blowing through the region before the Gadsden Purchase, however, as Anglo settlers began to arrive from the East. The first Anglos were stragglers, probably — a few mountain men on their way north to trap beavers on the Gila River, or small groups of pioneers who were traveling to California.

In 1846, the Mormon Battalion, a 397-member volunteer force led by Lieutenant Colonel Philip St. George Cooke, passed through Tucson. Although the United States and Mexico

(LEFT) *A dancer performs a Mexican folk dance at Tucson's Fourth Avenue Street Fair.* GILL C. KENNY (BELOW, LEFT) *A rider in the Fiesta de los Vaqueros rodeo parade carries a standard of the Virgin of Guadalupe.* EDWARD McCAIN (BELOW) *Mariachis entertain at numerous festivals and restaurants. Their instruments typically include trumpets, violins, guitars, and a bass guitar called a guitarrón.* GILL C. KENNY

were at war, the encounter was peaceful. The Mexican Army headed south out of harm's way. Meanwhile, Tucson residents were short on items of clothing, and the volunteer troopers were short on food; so soldiers and civilians swapped for what they needed.

A year later, another contact occurred between Mexican and American forces at Tucson, and this time there was some saber rattling by the U.S. troops. But the tiny outpost was an insignificant military prize, and a brief siege of the presidio soon was abandoned.

The gold rush in 1848 brought scores of travelers through Tucson. They were en route north along the Santa Cruz River to the Gila River, then west to the gold fields in California.

By most accounts Tucson was unattractive. Lieutenant Colonel Cooke noted, "Like Santa Fe ... its adobe houses are the same in appearance, but inferior." Most Easterners, unaccustomed to what they encountered in the West, described Tucson in disparaging terms: "dingy ... dilapidated ... forlorn ... godforsaken ... desolate ... dreary ... degraded ... barren ... baked and dried ... no great deal ... a miserable old place."

In 1880, the transcontinental railroad arrived, and everything changed. Until then, Tucson's shift from a mostly Mexican to a predominately Anglo population had been gradual. After the Gadsden Purchase in 1853, in which the United States bought land from Mexico, many Hispanic Tucsonenses moved back to Sonora, Mexico, but numerically Tucson remained a Mexican town until about 1910.

At the turn of the century, 4,122 of the 7,531 people who lived here were Hispanic. By 1920, the population had reached 20,337, of which 7,489 were Mexican-American; and at the start of World War II the number of Hispanic residents had declined to less than 30 percent of the city's population.

Today, with the interstate highway system and convenient air travel, it's

(LEFT) *The morning sun breaks through a clearing storm over the Rincon Mountains east of Tucson. Three other mountain ranges flank Tucson — the Santa Catalinas to the north, the Tucsons to the west, and the Santa Ritas far to the south.*
JACK DYKINGA
(ABOVE) *A number of Tucson's historic sites have been renovated for modern uses. This one, the Southern Pacific Railroad Station, now is a popular restaurant.*
GILL C. KENNY

Tucson offers a wide range of leisure activities. (ABOVE) *Golfers play on a variety of courses from desert to links nearly every day of the year in Tucson's warm, sunny climate.*
EDWARD MCCAIN
(BELOW) *Touring the Barrio Histórico includes viewing colorful murals depicting various aspects of Hispanic life in Tucson.*
GILL C. KENNY

hard to imagine what the Southern Pacific Railroad meant to Tucson more than 100 years ago. As local spectacle, it ranks with Lindbergh's solo flight across the Atlantic Ocean.

The railroad would put Tucson on the map. Excitement was so high that Mayor Bob Leatherwood penned a telegram to Pope Leo XIII to ask for his blessing. When the train finally arrived on March 20, 1880, crowds gathered, bands played, and an engraved silver spike was presented to Southern Pacific's president.

The railroad literally changed the face of Tucson. Within the railroad's first decade, bricks and lumber — too expensive to haul by wagon — began arriving on flatcars, and adobe virtually disappeared as a building material. North Main Avenue became a showcase of elegant homes with wide verandas fronted by expansive green lawns.

Laid across the city from west to east, the railroad effectively split Tucson, not just physically but also socially. Anglos lived on the north side, Hispanic residents on the south.

The railroad did indeed put Tucson on the map, and people from all over began to arrive. But it was not until after World War II that Tucson started becoming a Southwest metropolis.

Today, Tucson is a city of 700,000, a number that swells seasonally with the arrival in late fall of "snowbirds" from colder climates. Some come to play golf and participate in other recreation at destination resorts. A number of visitors are drawn by annual events, such as La Fiesta de los Vaqueros (the rodeo), Major League Baseball's spring training, or the Mariachi Conference.

Southeastern Arizona's natural wonders bring bird-watchers, hikers, rock climbers, and bicyclists. The good weather attracts runners and triathletes who train here in winter. And man-made wonders, such as the renowned Arizona-Sonora Desert Museum, Saguaro National Park, Kitt Peak National Observatory, Pima Air Museum, Titan Missile Museum, and the numerous wildlife preserves throughout southeastern Arizona, bring scores of visitors each year.

The city may have lost its predominately Hispanic face a long time ago, but its soul is still closely linked to its neighbor to the south, Sonora, Mexico.

That's evident in a number of ways. In some parts of town, Spanish is still the language of currency. In a moment of blatant civic pride, a former mayor once boasted that Tucson was the Mexican-food capital of the Southwest. And annually, the Mariachi Festival, Fiesta de San Agustín, Cinco de Mayo, and other Mexican fiestas bring crowds of celebrants to Tucson's streets and parks.

Anyone who takes the time to look can discover Tucson's Mexican, indeed its multi-ethnic, pedigree. One good way for a person to look is to tour one of the Old Pueblo's historic districts.

EL PRESIDIO
HISTORIC DISTRICT

With a self-guided walking tour map from the Metropolitan Tucson Convention & Visitors Bureau, I start my march through time at the Frémont House on the grounds of the Tucson Convention Center. The full name is Sosa-Carrillo-Frémont House. Members of the Sosa and Carrillo families were pioneers who preceded John Charles Frémont, the fifth territorial governor of Arizona, as occupants of the house. The adobe structure is typical of Tucson's architecture of territorial days.

José María Sosa III, a grandson of a soldier stationed at Presidio San Agustín del Tucson, was the first registered owner of this site. In 1878 the Carrillo family bought the property and built a home on it. That house, restored to the condition of Frémont's tenure, is the one that visitors see today.

After the Frémonts, a number of tenants rented the premises from the Carrillos. When most of Barrio Histórico was razed to clear the ground for the Convention Center, the Frémont House was saved, and later was purchased by the Arizona Historical Society. Now on the National Register

A setting sun and clouds paint a rainbow above the mosaic dome of the Pima County Courthouse in Tucson.
RANDY A. PRENTICE

DOWNTOWN SATURDAY NIGHT

I t's a familiar story. Shopping malls spring up on the city's outskirts, and the urban center, neglected, falls on hard economic times. Merchants liquidate or flee to the outskirts; stores close. Before long, empty show windows stare blindly into the noonday sun.

Vandalism comes next. Broken plate glass, architectural ornamentation stripped from facades, graffiti scrawled on walls — a definition of urban decay.

That's a picture of Congress Street in downtown Tucson 10 years ago.

Once a commercially prosperous district, the street had become a virtual skid row where the down and out slept on sidewalks outside run-down saloons. Even in daytime most people would avoid Congress Street between Stone and Fourth avenues. Nobody walked there alone at night.

But that was a decade ago. One recent Saturday night, as I stroll around, I find it difficult to recall the older, derelict street. Now, crowds surge along both sides of the street as entertainers perform. There's a rap group, jugglers and magicians, a jazz ensemble, dancers, a conga band, country and western singers, a one-man band, and a couple of rock bands.

Street artist and dancer Mitchell Kent spray paints a mural at Downtown Saturday Night, Tucson's biweekly arts festival and street fair.
EDWARD MCCAIN

In stalls set up inside the open-air Ronstadt Transportation Center, vendors sell leather goods, jewelry, carvings, and foodstuffs. On one street corner, a Bible-thumping evangelist, backed by an off-key gospel choir, exhorts the crowd to heed his doomsday sermon.

Galleries, specialty clothing stores, Southwest gift shops, import shops, coffee houses, chic secondhand stores, juice bars, jewelry shops, arty cafes — most of them closed by this time on weekday nights — are doing a lively trade this night.

A TV video crew interviews a shop owner for a local newscast, and in the background, filming the video crew with a hand-held movie camera, is a bunch of kids shooting a documentary.

Behind me I hear an unfamiliar accent and turn to face a man grinning from ear to ear, speaking to his wife in German. There are other tourists, of course, but most of the revelers are hometowners.

This is urban renewal in action. This is Downtown Saturday Night, a "community open house" that takes place along Congress Street on the first and third Saturdays of every month.

It's hard to pin down the inspirational sources for Downtown Saturday Night. Possibly the celebration started with a group of artists pooling their resources to open a storefront gallery where each could display his or her work.

To help draw patrons, musicians or performance artists sometimes appeared during evening hours. Maybe a coffee urn was installed in the back to bring in a little extra revenue. Then another group opened a second gallery down the block; a third followed and then a fourth.

Thus was born what is now officially called the Tucson Arts District. Its formation was endorsed by the Tucson City Council and led by the Tucson Arts District Partnership, a group incorporated to stimulate a revival of downtown. For information, call (520) 624-9977.

I meet some friends and we go to a cafe for coffee and pastry. The conversation turns to Tucson's reputation for nourishing the arts, including the performing arts: theater, dance, music.

We agree: Downtown Saturday Night was a great idea. ◪

of Historic Places, the home displays several period rooms furnished with belongings of its former residents.

From the Frémont House I walk north along Main Avenue to Washington Street, where a plaque marks the northwest corner of Tucson's original walled presidio. Just across Washington is an adobe building that was the original home of early entrepreneurs Sam and Atanacia Hughes. Now it is enlarged into a row of garden apartments. With the help of the guide map, I work my way south through the El Presidio District to the Tucson Museum of Art complex along Alameda Street.

Located in the complex, Casa Cordova, one of the oldest buildings in Tucson, dates to presidio days. Touring it provides a glimpse of life inside the walled presidio. One of the displays interprets artifacts dating from A.D. 700 to 900 — when Hohokam Indians occupied this site — through the 19th century.

I while away an afternoon exploring El Presidio and Barrio Histórico, two of the city's historic districts. Afterward, I walk to El Presidio Park, called Plaza de Las Armas in presidio days. Fiestas were celebrated on this site then, and still are today. Adjacent to the park, the Pima County Courthouse — with its fountain, tiled dome, columns, and archways — combines Spanish and Southwestern architectural styles. One exhibit there is part of the original presidio wall.

My last stop downtown is St. Augustine Cathedral on Stone Avenue. Built in 1896, it was remodeled in the late 1920s, when stained-glass windows, a sandstone facade, and towers were added. The church was enlarged again in the 1960s. Somewhat patterned after the Cathedral of Querétaro, Mexico, the church is celebrated for a bronze above its entry featuring St. Augustine and a saguaro, agave, and horned lizards of the Sonoran Desert.

Other historic neighborhoods in Tucson include Armory Park Historic District, near downtown, and Fort Lowell Historic District, on the east side. Like the Frémont House, the Fort Lowell site is a satellite of the Arizona Historical Society Museum.

For information and maps on the historic districts of Tucson, contact the Arizona Historical Society Museum, 949 East Second Street, Tucson, Arizona 85719; telephone (520) 628-5774; or the Metropolitan Tucson Convention & Visitors Bureau, 130 South Scott Avenue, Tucson, Arizona 85701; telephone (520) 624-1817.

UNIVERSITY OF ARIZONA

Local politics sure have been tame since the time delegate C.C. Stephens returned home from the 13th territorial legislative session, in which he had introduced a bill that established the Arizona Territorial University in Tucson. The year was 1885. What Tucson citizens had wanted Stephens to do was get the territorial capital back from Prescott where it had been moved eight years before. Failing that, there were other cuts of legislative pork to vie for: a normal school, a territorial prison,

(LEFT AND BELOW) *Restored and furnished in period antiques, the Sosa-Carrillo-Frémont House was for a time the home of American explorer and Arizona Territorial Governor John C. Frémont. Visitors today can tour the historic house near the Civic Center in downtown Tucson.*
JACK DYKINGA
GILL C. KENNY

even an insane asylum — anything but a university. In the whole territory there was not a single high school, for goodness sake. What was the city going to do with a university?

One saloon operator, it's claimed, pithily asserted his opposition on economic grounds: "Whoever heard of a professor buying a drink?"

Miffed Tucsonans talked about finding a more useful project — developing a water system, perhaps — for the Legislature's original university appropriation of $25,000, which depended, in any case, on the city's obtaining a 40-acre site for the school.

Finally, two gamblers and a saloon-keeper donated the requisite acreage, perhaps as a practical joke. The land was three miles from town and most citizens considered it worthless.

Despite these drawbacks, ground was broken. Six years later, on October 1, 1891, the University of Arizona opened its doors to 32 students, most of them high school students enrolled in a college-prep program. A little more than a century later, the university has 140 buildings on a campus encompassing 343 acres. And, it is the city's principal employer.

The university's accomplishments range from the Mirror Laboratory, where high-tech mirrors are manufactured for astronomy telescopes; to the invention of tree-ring dating, or dendrochronology, a technique indispensable to archaeology; to pioneering research in optical sciences, mechanical engineering, astronomy, arid lands studies, and anthropology.

FLANDRAU PLANETARIUM

Ever seen a kid totally engrossed in a game? Or in a zoo exhibit? Or in a demonstration? Multiply that by dozens of kids and you have an idea what the Flandrau Science Center and Planetarium is all about. When I walked in one Sunday afternoon, kids (and adults) were playing with pendulum games and balloons balanced over a column of air. They were absorbed in displays of lasers, or lined up for the asteroid walk-through or NASA space photographs.

The feature show in the planetarium that afternoon was called "Navajo Nights," a brilliant display of Navajo myths and legends surrounding the night sky.

A 16-inch telescope is available for viewing year-round on clear evenings. Laser shows on a variety of subjects and accompanied by music also are presented.

Flandrau is on the corner of Cherry and University on the University of Arizona campus. For information, telephone (520) 621-STAR.

ARIZONA HISTORICAL SOCIETY MUSEUM

Here's a little test, admittedly subjective, that I apply to museums: If it contains more interesting stuff than I can take in during a half-day's visit, it's a good museum. By that standard, the Arizona Historical Society's main museum, the oldest cultural institution in the state, ranks as outstanding.

The first afternoon on which I visited the museum, located at 949 East Second Street, between Park and Tyndall, I "got lost" in the "Arizona Mining Exhibit," which includes a replica of a turn-of-the-century underground copper mine, a blacksmith shop, assay office, stamp mill, and miner's tent. I got "unlost" only when

(BELOW) Visitors become the style — a shadow-casting arm — telling solar time on the Sidewalk Sundial at the University of Arizona's Flandrau Science Center and Planetarium.
FRANK ZULLO
(BOTTOM) Old Main, the first building on the UofA campus, is still in use.
GILL C. KENNY

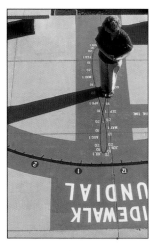

someone tapped me on the shoulder and gently informed me that it was closing time.

Other exhibits brought me back to the museum many times. One of them I'll always remember, particularly in early June when my backyard thermometer hovers above 100 degrees. It is the exhibit on the ingenious technologies that Arizonans have developed over the centuries to help tame the heat.

Other exhibits depict authentic period rooms from territorial days. The museum's library and archives are full of rare books, photos, maps, and historical documents.

For information, telephone (520) 628-5774.

ARIZONA STATE MUSEUM

Located just inside the main gate on the west side of the University of Arizona campus, the Arizona State Museum dates to territorial days, having been established in 1893 and, for decades, housed in the university's oldest building, Old Main.

In its current location, the museum collects and exhibits the archaeology, mineral wealth, and natural history of Arizona. One of the exhibits, "Paths of Life: American Indians of the Southwest," is a particularly fine example of this effort. Each of its 10 sections focuses on the origins, history, and present-day life of an Indian group.

For information, telephone (520) 621-6302.

CENTER FOR CREATIVE PHOTOGRAPHY

The roster of photographers represented at the Center for Creative Photography is extraordinary: Arbus, Weston, Lyon, White, Adams, Shahn, Dater, Siskind, Karsh, Cartier-Bresson, Steichen, Cunningham, Porter ... the list consists of one world-renowned photographer after another.

More than 1,400 photographers are represented in a collection of more than 60,000 images at the center, established in 1975 on the University of Arizona campus. Changing exhibits include photos from the center's permanent collections and traveling exhibitions. Print

The Arizona Historical Society interprets the cultures that left their marks on the state.
(ABOVE, LEFT) *A replica of a frontier copper mine delights students at the society's Arizona Heritage Center.*
JACK DYKINGA
(ABOVE) *A three-foot-tall santo, or carved wooden statue, of St. Augustine is displayed in an elaborately decorated setting complete with handmade paper flowers. The statue of Tucson's patron saint is a work of William Smith.*
DAVID BURCKHALTER

23

viewing from the archives is available on request. The center is on Olive Road near Speedway. For information, telephone (520) 621-7968.

ART MUSEUMS

Because space is limited, displays in the second-floor gallery at the University of Arizona Museum of Art are rotated about three times a year. Nearly three-fourths of the museum's holdings are in storage. These include an impressive collection of Renaissance art; the Gallagher Memorial Collection of more than 200 paintings, sculptures, and drawings by such notables as Degas, Rodin, and Picasso; and collected sculptural works of Jacques Lipchitz.

Located in the UofA art building on the corner of Park Avenue and Speedway Boulevard, the museum faces the pedestrian underpass on Olive Road. For information, telephone (520) 621-7567.

Downtown, at Alameda and Main streets, the display at the Tucson Museum of Art begins outdoors on the museum's north wall with two magnificent murals by Tucsonans Antonio Pazos and David Tineo. The tradition of wall painting goes back a thousand years in Hispanic culture; with nearly 140 murals throughout the city, the tradition is very strong in Tucson. The museum's permanent collection focuses on pre-Columbian art and on works from throughout the Americas. Also part of the permanent collection is the Campbell Gallery of Western Art.

For information, telephone (520) 624-2333.

BOTANICAL GARDENS

Desert dwellers love oases. One of my favorites is the Tucson Botanical Gardens, 5.5 acres of shade, tranquillity, and green in the heart of the city. That's gardens, plural, for the site consists of more than 15 plots with different themes.

A historical garden shows the kinds of plants brought to the region by the earliest settlers; a backyard bird garden displays plants to attract a variety of birds; a sensory garden invites visitors to touch, smell, and hear plants; a wildflower garden is splashed with the brilliance of poppies, marigolds, lupines, and other desert natives; and an Australian garden shows plants from Down Under that make attractive additions to Southwest gardens.

For information, telephone (520) 326-9686. Or write to the Tucson Botanical Gardens, 2150 North Alvernon Way, Tucson, Arizona 85712.

TOHONO CHUL PARK

In the language of the Desert People, the Tohono O'odham Indians, *tohono chul* means "desert corner."

A private 37-acre park near the northwest corner of Oracle and Ina roads is exactly that — a pristine piece of Sonoran Desert. An inner trail system in Tohono Chul links exhibits within the park while an outer-loop trail leads through unspoiled desert.

More than 15 species of birds are permanent residents in this desert corner, which features arid-lands plants from Arizona, Texas, and Mexico as well as exhibits on animals, fish, geology, and plants used by native cultures of the Southwest.

A tea room and garden cafe at Tohono Chul serve breakfast, lunch, and afternoon tea. For information, telephone (520) 575-8468.

REID PARK ZOO

The zoo is the centerpiece of the Gene C. Reid Park in central Tucson and features exotic species native to Africa, Australia, Asia — even polar regions.

Two 18-hole public golf courses, picnic areas, a band shell, swimming pool, tennis courts, and a small fishing lake are among the other attractions at the park, located at 900 South Randolph Way, off 22nd Street between Country Club Road and Alvernon Way.

Hi Corbett Field, adjacent to the park, is the spring-training site of the Major League Colorado Rockies.

For park information, call (520) 791-3204 or 791-4022. ◆

The Tucson Museum of Art blends art, architecture and history in its five-block complex that includes the museum, restored houses from the city's original presidio, and a plaza. The museum features changing exhibits as well as permanent exhibits of pre-Columbian and Western art.
GILL C. KENNY

Most of central Tucson's attractions are within a short drive of each other, and good restaurants abound. Allow a half-hour drive into town from the outlying resorts and hotels.

Pick up your free guide pamphlet for the **Downtown Walking Tour** at the Metropolitan Tucson Convention & Visitors Bureau, 130 South Scott Avenue, and take half a day to explore the city's roots. There are a number of places to eat — from hot dog carts to fine Mexican food — along the route.

Allow half a day or more for your trip back in time at the **Arizona Historical Society Museum**, 949 East Second Street, telephone (520) 628-5774.

Wandering desert walkways amid the incredible variety of plants at **Tucson Botanical Gardens**, 2150 North Alvernon Way, will take at least two hours.

A half-day or more should give you a good look at African elephants, giraffes, and other animals at the **Reid Park Zoo**. The entrance is on Lakeshore Drive off 22nd Street, just east of Country Club Road. The zoo is open 9 A.M. to 4 P.M. every day except Christmas. There is a snack bar on the premises and there are a number of restaurants nearby. Telephone (520) 791-3204.

Touring the **University of Arizona** campus can take from two hours to all day, depending upon which attractions you choose to take in. Eat at nearby off-campus restaurants or at the student union.

Take at least an hour to explore the **Flandrau Science Center and Planetarium** on campus. It provides an impressive mineral display, star shows, laser shows, and more. Schedules of shows vary daily.

The **Arizona State Museum** will enthrall you for at least two hours.

At the **Center for Creative Photography**, 1030 North Olive Road, Building 3, set your exposure for at least two hours of great photography. Explore their website at http://www.ccp.arizona.edu/ccp.html.

The historic Hotel Congress in downtown Tucson anchors the city's burgeoning arts district. Reflecting the recent resurgence of downtown, the Congress has been refurbished, and it serves as a meeting place for Tucson's artists.
EDWARD MCCAIN

❶ Arizona Historical Society

❷ Arizona State Museum

❸ Center for Creative Photography

❹ Flandrau Planetarium

❺ Reid Park Zoo

❻ Tucson Botanical Gardens

TUCSON'S PERIMETER

THE TRAILS LEAD TO BACKCOUNTRY, SACRED INDIAN SITES, AND URBAN ACTIVITIES

Chapter 2

Afriend of mine on a visit from "back East," as we 12-year Arizona "natives" love to say, once sat in my living room and contemplated the number of days he could spend in Tucson without running out of new things to do,

either in town or on its perimeter. "Let's see," he said, "tomorrow the Desert Museum — that'll take a day — then there's the Arizona Ballet tomorrow night. A hike into the Rincon Mountains on Saturday and a stroll through the Arts District during Downtown Saturday Night. Then there's Mount Lemmon, historic districts, the Arizona State Museum ...."

He isn't a spectator-sports guy, so he didn't mention baseball spring training or the sports offerings at the University of Arizona. His list did include El Tour de Tucson, one of the biggest perimeter bicycle races in the world, and outings in the Santa Catalina, Rincon, and Tucson mountains.

Although I agree with most of the points on my friend's list, his and mine

wouldn't necessarily be the same. Here's my sampling of things to see and do in the Tucson area:

THE MOUNTAINS

With its mountains — the Santa Catalinas to the north, the Rincons to the east, the smaller but impressive Tucson Mountains to the west — Tucson is blessed. Years ago, right after I arrived in Tucson, a friend told me that the city's best feature was its quick access to the backcountry.

"I know only a few other places like Tucson," he said. "You can park your car at Sabino Canyon, take one of several trails that go into the Catalinas, and hike for days without ever retracing your steps." When he moved to the city

(Opposite page) Ancient petroglyphs, rock carvings that send enigmatic messages across the centuries, decorate a boulder at Saguaro National Park near Tucson. A protected stand of saguaro cacti lies in the background.
DAVID MUENCH
(Above) A summer storm strikes Tucson near sunset.
BRUCE GRIFFIN

(ABOVE) *Rock climbers Jim Cronk and Bob Kerry test their skills on Mount Lemmon's Goosehead Rock.* RANDY A. PRENTICE (ABOVE, RIGHT) *Hikers admire the spectacle of Seven Falls in the Santa Catalina Mountains' Bear Canyon.* EDWARD MCCAIN (OPPOSITE PAGE) *Autumn paints Sabino Canyon in the Santa Catalinas.* RANDY A. PRENTICE

a few years before, he was so eager to experience this feature that he set off in the middle of winter, snowshoes lashed to the top of his backpack, and camped alone high in the Santa Catalinas for a week and a half.

Not quite up to such adventures myself, I joined the Southern Arizona Hiking Club, and with companions hiked the many trails originating in the lower Sabino Canyon Recreation Area.

There's the Bear Canyon Trail, sometimes called the Seven Falls Trail for the magnificent waterfalls a couple of miles up. Beyond the falls, the trail branches onto the Palisade Trail, which goes to the ranger station among the pines. There's the Phoneline Trail. It winds high along the canyon's walls to merge with the Sabino Canyon Trail, then connects to either the Box Camp Trail or the West Fork Sabino Trail. Take a slightly different turn from the parking

lot and you're on the Esperero Canyon Trail heading up to Bridal Veil Falls and on to Cathedral Rock.

What my friend said about Sabino Canyon is true, of course, but it's also true, on a smaller scale, of other canyons accessible from the Tucson side of the Santa Catalinas: Ventana, Pima, Romero, and Finger Rock canyons.

Hiking in the Catalinas, I often feel I'm walking in very old footprints. Like a lot of other well-watered canyons in southeastern Arizona's sky-island mountain ranges, Sabino Canyon has been a desert oasis for thousands of years. These trails are as old as the animals that wore them in before early people ground acorn kernels to powder in metates (bowl-shaped grinding stones) or roamed into the canyon's upper reaches to hunt game.

SABINO CANYON

The lure of water in the desert is strong. People come to the Sabino Canyon oasis to observe animal and bird life. After summer thunderstorms, people flock to deep pools for a cooling dip or to sunbathe on warm rocks. Holiday weekends bring scores of picnickers to the canyon. Daily, buses shuttle tourists four miles up the paved canyon road. The more ambitious recreationists, of course, will hike to secluded pools in the higher elevations. Trout fishermen, too, favor the deeper pools in the Catalinas, even if getting to them requires climbing over midstream boulders the size of pickup trucks.

In winter, ice and snow elsewhere in the West bring rock climbers to the sheer granite faces at Windy Point along the Mount Lemmon Highway. And daily in good weather, bicycle racers train on the highway's 26-mile climb.

Summer and winter, the aptly named community of Summerhaven, some 8,000 feet high in the Santa Catalina Mountains, is a getaway for desert city dwellers. Temperatures atop the mountain may be 25 degrees cooler than in Tucson, so in summer Mount Lemmon Highway is often crowded with cars carrying picnickers and hikers. Above Summerhaven, Ski Valley offers winter recreation, but snow this far south is undependable even at higher elevations, so there are years when the ski slopes are open for only a few days.

Unlike access to the Catalinas, there are no improved roads in the Rincon Mountains, southeast of the Catalinas. Either you walk in or you ride a horse.

In early spring one year, I backpacked to Manning Camp, high among Rincon Mountain pines. On the way up I met three hikers descending. Once I reached the summit, though, I hiked from my base camp for five days without seeing another soul.

COLOSSAL CAVE

Southeast from Tucson follow Old Spanish Trail to the front gates of a popular tourist site — Colossal Cave and its accompanying park, picnic grounds, campsites, and gift shop. Formed from limestone, it is one of the world's largest dry caverns.

Guides who conduct a 45-minute tour of the cave love to regale visitors with a tale of a train robber named Phil Carver, who supposedly cached $62,000 in gold in the cave in 1879. After serving a long term in Yuma prison, Carver, it is said, returned to the cave and disappeared. All that aside, the cave's best features are beautiful limestone stalagmites, stalactites, and columns.

For more directions and admission information, telephone (520) 647-7275.

CATALINA STATE PARK

Just a few miles north of Tucson on State Route 77 (Oracle Road), Catalina State Park protects and interprets 5,500 acres of high desert in the foothills of the Santa Catalina Mountains. Except for the Nature Trail, the park's trails are open to horses, and a parking area with corrals has been set aside for equestrians. Campsites are available on a first-come, first-served basis.

Just south of the park looms rugged Pusch Ridge, a refuge for a small herd of desert bighorn sheep and a nesting site for peregrine falcons.

From the park, the Romero Canyon Trail takes hikers to a number of streams and pools in the Pusch Ridge Wilderness. The trail intersects with others in the wilderness and adjoining areas.

For more information, telephone (520) 628-5798.

29

PICACHO PEAK

Early each spring I call my wild-flower contacts at the Arizona-Sonora Desert Museum and elsewhere in the state to find out what's in bloom and where to find it. Picacho Peak State Park, north of Tucson, is usually on my checklist. In a good year the slopes are blanketed with Mexican poppies. It's one of the best places I know to see spring flowers.

Most flower-watchers, I'd guess, will not know that the Civil War came to Arizona right near here. On April 15, 1862, Union soldiers from California clashed with Confederate forces on the march from Tucson. Five men were killed in the Battle at Picacho Pass, the westernmost skirmish of the Civil War. When I think of that fight, I wonder if the poppies were in bloom that spring.

Picacho Peak provides an excellent overview of classic desert terrain. The 2.5-mile trail has a short, steep climb near the top that requires hikers to hold onto steel-cable handrails. But the 360-degree views from the peak's 3,374-foot summit make the climb, and the scariness, worthwhile.

Picacho Peak State Park is 40 miles north of Tucson on I-10, with 95 campsites, showers, and dump site available. For information, telephone (520) 466-3183.

(LEFT) *Yucca and cholla thrive in the desert grasslands below Pusch Ridge at Catalina State Park on the road to Oracle.* JACK DYKINGA

(ABOVE) *Spring brings an impressive display of poppies to Picacho Peak State Park along Interstate 10 north of Tucson.* P.K. WEIS

EL TOUR DE TUCSON

In 1983, Richard DeBernadis, himself an enthusiastic perimeter bicyclist, invited the entire community to bike a 111-mile circuit around Tucson, an event which became El Tour de Tucson.

Now, each November on the Saturday before Thanksgiving, more than 3,000 riders of all ages and every level of expertise pedal out at staggered starts to complete 25, 50, 75, or the full 111 miles.

Despite the family atmosphere, as one of the top-10 perimeter bike races in the world, El Tour de Tucson draws top cyclists from everywhere. Overall, the event has raised more than $3.9 million for local and national charities. For more information on El Tour de Tucson and other perimeter bicycling events in Arizona, telephone (520) 745-2033.

DESERT MUSEUM

Since it opened in 1952, the Arizona-Sonora Desert Museum has carried out a unique mission: to exhibit only plants and animal species native to the Sonoran Desert and its contiguous habitats. Nothing exotic.

Visitors to the museum encounter the very things they see on their drive from Tucson west across Gates Pass in the Tucson Mountains and on down to the museum grounds in Tucson Mountain Park.

The difference is that the museum presents birds and mammals and desert plants in interpretive settings that shed light on the Sonoran Desert's marvelous biodiversity.

Still, birds and bighorn sheep occupied spaces of their own; mountain lions had another space, and prairie dogs still another.

As time passed, the museum improved exhibits by developing enclosures that resembled natural habitats.

Trouble was, reptiles, birds, amphibians, and mammals were exhibited as if they lived apart from each other. This was a false picture of nature.

But things are changing. Working from a plan that will take 10 years or longer to implement, the museum staff is developing exhibits that emphasize communities of plants and animals, not just individual ones. The idea is to show how life forms dependent on each other share a habitat.

"When it's finished, we'll probably start over," says museum director David Hancocks. "These long-range plans are not forever."

The newer museum exhibits create the impression that you are actually inside a desert biome, not on the outside looking in. And the parts of each exhibit fit together in such a way as to tell a story about the plants and animals that share a particular environmental niche.

The mountain islands exhibit is a good example of where all this planning and development is heading. The exhibit opened in 1986, but already is scheduled for renovation. In fact, director Hancocks anticipates, all the new exhibits will require post-installation tinkering and fine-tuning, and — more than likely — eventual remodeling.

The idea of the mountain habitat is to show the transition from desert to

(BELOW, LEFT) At the world-renowned Arizona-Sonora Desert Museum, a stroll of a little more than 50 yards transports visitors through all the life zones that occur in southern Arizona and northern Mexico — from desert to alpine. (BELOW, RIGHT) An ocelot peers from a cave within its habitat at the museum.
BOTH BY MARTY CORDANO

grassland to wooded mountain elevations, and to illustrate how southeastern Arizona's sky islands function in relation to other biomes.

Perennial streams flow in many of southeastern Arizona's mountains, so one of the first sounds you'll hear as you enter the museum's sky-island exhibit is water trickling from a small spring. Steller's jays scold intruders, black bears and wolves roam woodland enclosures, and a mountain lion sleeps beneath a shaded ledge.

As you exit the sky-island region, you begin to descend along a path that seems to follow the switchback contours of a mountain trail. You are moving through a Transition Zone so gradually that you're scarcely aware of having left the Mountain Life Zone.

Looking up and around, you see a new vegetative regime — plants typical of rolling grasslands in mountain foothills. There are grama grasses, clumps of bear grass, agave, yucca, ocotillo, and sotol.

Suddenly, you realize that you have moved into another habitat. It's the desert grasslands, an exhibit completed in 1993.

Ideally, that's the way it's supposed to go. The museum seeks to create an illusion that you're not meandering through a zoo, but through a series of wild parks, so to speak — moving from Arizona upland through mountain and grassland habitats, then on to the tropical deciduous forest land, the Baja Peninsula, and the lower Colorado habitat.

The museum is 14 miles west of Tucson. Drive west on Speedway Boulevard, and follow the signs across Gates Pass. Caution: Trucks, vehicles towing trailers, and RVs are prohibited on Gates Pass. Drivers of these vehicles should take Ajo Road west to Kinney Road, and then north to the museum.

The museum charges an admission fee. Hours in winter are 8:30 A.M. to 5 P.M.; in summer they are 7:30 A.M. to 6 P.M. The museum is open every day of the year, including holidays. No pets are allowed on the museum grounds. The facility is wheelchair accessible. Telephone (520) 883-1380.

The Arizona-Sonora Desert Museum enables visitors to immerse themselves in the Sonoran Desert and learn about the environment that many people live in but often know little about. (ABOVE) A tarantula spider delights a future wildlife biologist. While they are venomous and frightening in appearance, tarantulas have a gentle nature and seldom bite unless they are provoked. CHRISTINE KEITH (LEFT) The mammoth exhibit chronicles the disappearance of the largest mammal to roam the region's grasslands. MARTY CORDANO

OLD TUCSON

On a morning drive out Speedway toward Gates Pass, I spotted a guy thumbing a ride. He wore a high-peaked, ten-gallon Western hat, cowboy boots, fringed buckskin chaps, and a greatcoat, buttoned almost to his knees. "What the devil," I said aloud.

Cautiously, I slowed to a stop. "Thank heaven," he said as he hopped in before I could ask his destination. "I thought no one was going to stop."

"It's no wonder, with that get-up you're wearing," I said. "Where are you headed?"

He grinned. "My name's Bill. I'm late. I was supposed to be at Old Tucson an hour ago for a movie I'm acting in. A little too much partying last night, I guess." He grinned again.

I wanted to ask why a movie actor had to hitchhike to the set, but I didn't. Bill, it turned out, was employed at Old Tucson Studios. Compact and athletic, he was the guy who gets shot off a roof and tumbles to the street in staged shoot-outs that are part of daily shows.

The movie in which he was playing a bit part was the Western comedy *Three Amigos*, as I recall. That was a few years back, so I don't know if Bill still does his tumbling act for tourists at Old Tucson.

Old Tucson, now a Western theme park and major tourist attraction, was originally a set for the movie *Arizona*, filmed in 1939. Since then it has been used as a location for numerous films and TV series. Its dirt streets, boardwalks, and adobe buildings are a reproduction of 1860s Tucson. A stagecoach, narrow-gauge train, and carousel are among the rides available to visitors. A gift shop, restaurant, saloon, and Iron Door Mine are available for tours.

Old Tucson has undergone some changes since a 1995 fire forced it to close temporarily and rebuild. Sound stage tours may be no longer on the bill, but there are more live shows and staged shoot-outs than ever. The Town Hall Museum offers western history and mineral exhibits, plus Arizona's history in the movies.

Old Tucson is 12 miles west of Tucson. Take Speedway Boulevard west and follow the signs across Gates Pass. Trucks, vehicles hauling trailers, and RVs must take I-10 to I-19 south, take the Ajo Way exit west to Kinney Road, and then follow the signs. Admission fee. Hours: 10 A.M. to 6 P.M. daily, year round, except Thanksgiving and Christmas. For information, telephone (520) 883-0100.

TUCSON MOUNTAINS

Along Gates Pass Road west of Tucson there's a traffic pullout where a large sign posts park rules. "Park rules?" I remember asking the first time I saw that sign, "What park?"

The park in question is called Tucson Mountain Park, an 11,000-acre Arizona uplands park run by the Pima County Parks and Recreation Department. Thousands of visitors annually pass through the park without realizing it. Usually they are on their way to the Arizona-Sonora Desert Museum or Old Tucson, both located within the park, or to Saguaro National Park West, which is adjacent to it. But Tucson Mountain Park is known to regular winter visitors who camp in its Gilbert Ray Campground. And the park certainly is well-known to local outdoor enthusiasts who use its hiking, equestrian, and mountain-bike trails.

Many of the trails will take you to Wasson Peak, the highest point in the Tucson Mountains. There's the King Canyon Trail, directly across from the Desert Museum parking lot; the Hugh Norris Trail on Bajada Loop Drive west of Saguaro National Park; the Esperanza

Now in its sixth decade, Old Tucson has entertained millions of Old West fans on film and with live action. (BELOW) A visitor learns from a stunt man the fine art of faking a right hook. (BOTTOM) Actor Lou Diamond Phillips herds cattle through "town" for the movie Young Guns II. BOTH BY EDWARD McCAIN

Trail on the mountain's north side; and the Sweetwater Canyon Trail on the northeast approach. The trails vary in length, so you can pick one for your own fitness level. Trail- guide pamphlets are available at Saguaro National Park headquarters.

I avoid Tucson Mountain Park in summer, when daytime temperatures frequently exceed 100° Fahrenheit, but hike its trails often during winter, spring, and fall. No time is prettier than early spring for hiking in the mountain park.

Some friends and I once celebrated spring's advent by hitting the King Canyon Trail an hour before dawn on the morning of the vernal equinox. A slice of moon lighted our path and only the steady crunch of gravel underfoot broke the silence.

As dawn came on, the breeze freshened and we heard the wind whispering across the stiff spines of saguaro cacti. Familiar shapes began to emerge from the gray light: ocotillo, jojoba, and barrel cacti. Taller saguaros swayed in the breeze.

A curve-billed thrasher, the earliest morning caller, whistled. When the first rosy hues painted the nearby ridges, a chorus of song greeted the dawn — the descending trill of a canyon wren, the rolling churr of a Gila woodpecker, a cardinal, and the improbable chugging of a cactus wren. After a couple of miles we came to a low saddle where we rested and snacked.

I often boast that there is no month in these mountains when you won't see a flower in bloom. So far, the flower goddesses of the Tucson Mountains have not let me down. Approaching the saddle, we saw desert hyacinth, chia, fairy duster, and filaree. As we climbed toward Wasson Peak, we saw bright patches of Mexican poppies, marigold, globe mallow, and penstemon.

From the saddle the trail rises steeply toward the central ridge of the range. From vantage points along the switchback trail we looked back to the Arizona-Sonora Desert Museum, beyond to the broad sweep of the Avra and Altar valleys. In the distance we saw the white-mantled telescopes atop Kitt Peak.

At 4,687 feet, Wasson Peak yields one of the best scopes of southeastern Arizona's basin-and-range province. On a clear day I have counted more than 15 mountain ranges, from the Superstition Mountains east of Phoenix to the Tohono O'odham Indians' sacred Baboquivari

(ABOVE, LEFT) *Arcing ribs of a dead saguaro frame the foothills at Tucson Mountain Park.* EDWARD MCCAIN
(ABOVE) *Hikers explore the Hugh Norris Trail in the Tucson Mountains.* PETER KRESAN

Peak, located south of Kitt Peak near the border with Mexico.

SAGUARO NATIONAL PARK

In June — although sometimes as early as mid-May — the saguaro cacti that grow in dense forests on the fan-shaped *bajadas* of the Tucson Mountains and in the foothills of the Catalinas and Rincons begin to display coronets of creamy white flowers. The white-winged dove and the long-nosed bat, both of which winter in Mexico and are chief pollinators of the saguaro blossom, seem to time their return to correspond with the flowering of this giant cactus.

The juicy, scarlet fruit pulps are a favorite snack of scores of birds and of some mammals lucky enough to scavenge fallen ones. Traditionally, the Tohono O'odham Indians harvest the fruits by using long poles to poke them from their crown-like settings. Sometimes the fruits are fermented into a drink used in a rain-making ceremony.

Tucson's cross-town units of Saguaro National Park — Saguaro East in the foothills of the Rincon Mountains and Saguaro West in the Tucson Mountains — contain two of the finest saguaro stands anywhere in Arizona. Of course, there's much more to see in the two units than saguaros. Each is a prime

Saguaro National Park preserves the natural wonders of the Sonoran Desert. (ABOVE, RIGHT) *A Harris' hawk perches atop saguaro cacti blossoms.* JOHN CANCALOSI. (BELOW) *Run-off from winter rains produces ephemeral cascades.* RANDY A. PRENTICE (OPPOSITE PAGE) *A mule deer ambles up a desert wash.* TOM DANIELSEN

example of the Arizona upland region of the Sonoran Desert.

The older of the two units, Saguaro East, offers a nine-mile paved loop for motorists and bicyclists, with picnic areas along the way. The unit is located on Old Spanish Trail five miles east of Broadway. There is an admission fee. Backcountry permits for overnight trips may be obtained free of charge at the visitors center.

Saguaro West harbors the six-mile unpaved Bajada Loop Drive that provides access to hiking trails and picnic areas. The unit is located on North Kinney Road two miles northwest of the Arizona-Sonora Desert Museum. There is no admission charge at Saguaro West. Visitors center hours at both units are 8 A.M. to 5 P.M. daily. For information, telephone (520) 733-5100 or the visitors centers, (520) 733-5153 (East) and 733-5158 (West).

Note: No water is available at either unit except at the visitors centers.

KITT PEAK AND BABOQUIVARI

The landmarks are familiar sites visible from Wasson Peak, the Arizona-Sonora Desert Museum, and from many high places on trails in nearby mountain ranges. The one is a monument to science; the other is sacred ground to the Tohono O'odham Indians. The first is an array of gleaming white housings for more than a dozen telescopes; the second is a jagged granite pinnacle pointing skyward. Few visitors to the site are aware that the sacred and the scientific are intertwined at the observatories on Kitt Peak at the eastern edge of the Papago Indian Reservation, southwest of Tucson. Driving to the 7,000-foot summit on

BIOSPHERE 2 CENTER

What strikes me first about the Biosphere 2, nestled in the Santa Catalina foothills near Oracle, Arizona, is how much it resembles a college campus. Spacious lawns separate clusters of buildings, a small tree-lined brook runs through the center of the grounds, and beneath a fig tree, I spot a student stuffing ripe figs into his daypack.

Biosphere 2 is indeed a campus — the Western Campus of Columbia University's Earth Institute — with a distinguished faculty in Earth Sciences and students enrolled for university credit. The campus centerpiece is Biosphere 2 itself, a 7.2-million-cubic-foot glass-and-steel spaceframe that shelters seven miniature ecosystems: a savanna, fresh and saltwater marshes, a tropical rainforest, a desert, a 900,000-gallon self-sustaining ocean, and an agricultural bay. Envisioned as a laboratory for studying life in an enclosed, self-sustaining world, Biosphere 2 was finished in 1991, and eight "biospherians" shut themselves in to grow their own food, recycle wastes, purify water, and breathe oxygen produced by plants.

But nature can be perverse, even

inside a giant terrarium. Oxygen levels plummeted, crops failed, and birds, animals, and insects died off. Its managers were ridiculed for practicing sham science at just another commercial tourist attraction.

After Columbia University's Earth Institute took over Biosphere 2's programs in 1996, the complex was renamed Columbia University Biosphere 2 Center. Today, Biosphere 2 specializes in studying the effects of increased carbon dioxide in a carefully regulated environment. The idea of putting people inside for sustained periods was abandoned, and the former Human Habitat, now sealed off from the installation's other biomes, was opened to the public.

We begin our tour at the Visitor Center, strolling around a scale model of the complex before viewing a short documentary film. Then we're on the move, descending paved walkways to the biome demonstration laboratories, small-scale duplicates of larger biomes within Biosphere 2.

Since visitors are not permitted to enter Biosphere 2 itself, the demonstration labs provide a simulation of life inside. From the tropical rain forest, abloom with exotic flowers, we walk through the transitional thorn scrub and savanna, the coastal fog desert, a rice paddy and fish farm, and finally, the desert biome.

After a refreshment stop and cyber tour at the Cyber Café, we approach the "big house." We peer through its soaring glass panels into rainforest, marsh, and desert biomes. Then we enter the Human Habitat.

The ocean, real waves lapping at its tiny shores, is our last stop. From the underwater gallery, we view fishes, plants, corals, and other undersea life.

The Biosphere 2 campus also offers a hotel, conference center, gift shops, and restaurant. For information, telephone (520) 896-6200 or (800) 828-2462 (their Web site's address is www.bio2.edu). ⚘

(BELOW) The recognizable glass domes of Biosphere 2 now form a university campus, but does anyone know what Biosphere 1 is? That's the Earth, of course.
PETER ENSENBERGER

the winding, 12-mile mountain road off State Route 86, tourists can't miss the odd-shaped, bald outcropping jutting straight up several miles south. They frequently stop by the roadside to peer through binoculars at its rough outlines. Some will have identified it on maps and will know its name, Baboquivari, but not its meaning. A few will know that to get here they crossed lands of those who call themselves Tohono O'odham, "desert people," without whose permission there would be no telescopes on Kitt Peak.

Baboquivari Peak got its English name via a Spanish rendering of *waw kiwulk* — an O'odham word that roughly translates as "hill squeezed in the middle," as if the hand of its maker pinched and twisted it slightly before the clay hardened. For nearly a century, Baboquivari's nearly vertical exposures have challenged rock climbers. Among the few who have climbed its most difficult route all the way to its 7,730-foot summit was the late U. S. Supreme Court Justice William O. Douglas.

To many of the Tohono O'odham, Baboquivari is the center of the universe and home of their most important deity, I'itoy (Elder Brother), the creator of human beings. In the beginning, according to O'odham teachings, there was Coyote, Buzzard, and I'itoy. In time, other powerful beings came into existence, one of whom was Siwani, who came from the north to fight with I'itoy.

On four consecutive nights they fought, and each time I'itoy was killed. The first three times, he came back to life with the dawn, but on the fourth night he stayed dead. Eventually his bones were scattered across the landscape. After many years, I'itoy returned in the shape of an old man wandering from village to village searching for allies to help him fight Siwani once again. No one would volunteer.

Finally he was joined by people from the underworld and with their help he conquered Siwani. These helpers, the ancestors of the Tohono O'odham, then moved out of the underworld to live on the desert near Baboquivari. And I'itoy retired to a cave in the mountain, where he still lives.

His reappearances among the desert people are rare; only when calamity threatens does I'itoy come down from his cave. He returned when the monster Nehbig, who sucked up whole villages and devoured them, was loose on the land. Another time he was needed to help kill Ho'ok, the witch who ate children. In modern times, when the railroad was being built across the O'odham reservation, I'itoy came down from his cave to move animals to safety.

Understandably, the Tohono O'odham were far from enthusiastic about Kitt Peak's selection as the site for a national observatory. But eventually the tribal council approved an agreement that would grant Kitt Peak to the national observatory for as long as the installation was used for astronomy.

The first stop for visitors atop Kitt Peak is the visitors center and museum, where a video presentation and a number of exhibits feature astronomy. One of the first things that caught my attention was a couple of computer terminals just inside the entrance where visitors can test their knowledge of astronomy by taking an on-screen, multiple-choice test. If you do halfway well, messages pop up to encourage you to go on: "Wow! You really know your astronomy," flashed on the screen after I had answered three in a row correctly. "Carl Sagan, eat your heart out!" was another.

I picked up a pamphlet from a rack at the visitors center and set off on a self-guided walking tour. Guided tours also are offered, but I prefer to see things at my own pace. The highlight of my walking tour was the Mayall four-meter telescope. The day was bright and clear, and from the Mayall visitors gallery 96 feet above the mountaintop, I could see more than a hundred miles in every direction.

Afterward, I drove to Kitt Peak's picnic area, where I ate a sack lunch and wandered among scrub oaks, juniper, and piñon. The most conspicuous of the many birds flitting about in the picnic

The four-meter Mayall telescope, one of the world's largest, surveys the cloudless Arizona heavens from Kitt Peak, 60 miles west of Tucson.
RANDY A. PRENTICE

Mission San Xavier del Bac, the finest example of Spanish mission architecture in the United States, has served the faithful for nearly 300 years. Established by Padre Eusebio Francisco Kino in 1700, the mission buildings standing today were begun in 1783.
JACK DYKINGA

grounds were sassy gray-breasted jays. While I ate, two landed on my picnic table and pecked at the piece of bread crust I offered.

Kitt Peak is open to the public from 9 A.M. to 4 P.M. daily except Thanksgiving, December 24 and 25, and January 1. Guided tours, for which a donation is suggested, are offered weekdays at 11 A.M., 1 P.M., and 2:30 P.M. On weekends an additional tour starts at 9:30 A.M. For information on night tours, contact: Public Information Office, National Optical Astronomy Observatories, P.O. Box 26732, Tucson, Arizona 85726. Call (520) 318-8726 or 318-8200.

SAN XAVIER MISSION

It's a church, not a historical museum. That's the first thing to be said about Mission San Xavier del Bac, 10 miles south of downtown Tucson on the San Xavier Indian Reservation.

Worshipers arrive daily to celebrate Mass or to light a candle and kneel before the reclining figure of the mission's patron, St. Francis Xavier. Sometimes sick people or relatives of the ill pin notes or replicas of afflicted body parts to the saint's garments. For almost 300 years, since 1700 when Padre Eusebio Francisco Kino ordered the foundations laid, the faithful have come to mission churches at the village of Bac.

Father Kino envisioned a magnificent church with a courtyard and running water supplied by the nearby Rio Santa Cruz. But before he could realize his dream, he was called back to Mission Dolores in Sonora. Other Jesuits followed Kino and a succession of churches were erected at Bac, but the splendid combination of Spanish Colonial, Moorish, and Byzantine architectural styles that occupies the site today was begun by Franciscan missionaries in 1783.

What many believe to be the finest example of mission architecture in the United States was renovated in the 1990s by an international team of preservationists led by conservators from the Guggenheim Museum in New York City.

Completed in 1997, the renovation painstakingly removed grime from the church's interior artwork. Thousands of votive candles burned over the centuries left behind thick coatings of soot. At the same time, damage to the mission's exterior, some of it unwittingly caused by previous attempts at preservation, was repaired.

On a Sunday afternoon visit in March, while the renovation was going on, I was struck by just how much Mission San Xavier is still a community church. The occasion was the 12th annual Wa:k Powwow.

Wa:k, "where the water rises from the ground," is the O'odham word from which the Spanish Bac is derived. Powwow is an Indian festival featuring singing, dancing, and drumming.

Tourists walked among booths set up in the parking area. Indians from more than 20 Western tribes sold arts and crafts. The powwow grounds were in a large, open area behind the church where bleachers had been set up around a dance arena.

Every few minutes a new group of dancers would enter the arena. There were dances for men and women alone, dances for pairs and teams, even open dances for all comers.

As I watched a dance performed by lovely young women garbed in buckskin, I felt a tap on my shoulder. A girl of 12 offered candy bars. "They're 50 cents apiece," she said, "to help our church." A smiling nun stood behind the girl.

"It's for the restoration," she explained.

You can visit the mission any time, but the church and gift shop are open from 8 A.M. to 6 P.M. Donations are requested for the ongoing renovation. For more information and a Mass schedule, telephone (520) 294-2624.

To find San Xavier Mission, take I-19 south to Exit 91, San Xavier Road. The mission is about a half-mile west.

AIR & SPACE MUSEUM

Several years ago I took an out-of-town guest to the Pima Air & Space Museum. He's what I'd refer to, without sarcasm, as an airplane nut. At the sight of all those rows of airplanes parked and

(ABOVE) *Many hand-carved statues of saints and other holy figures occupy niches throughout the ornately decorated San Xavier del Bac Mission.* WILLARD CLAY (BELOW) *Built near the banks of the Santa Cruz River, San Xavier ministers to the Tohono O'odham Indians, who farmed extensively along the river centuries before Europeans came to the New World.* GILL C. KENNY

waiting, he began rapidly patting his chest in imitation of his racing heart.

After paying your admission, the first thing you walk into is a 20,000-square-foot hall of airplanes and related objects. This building and other hangars on the grounds house one of the three largest collections of historic aircraft in the world. Someone like my friend could spend a day at the museum in one exhibit hall alone.

But that's only the beginning. Outside, there are acres of airplanes: fighters, bombers, helicopters, cargo planes, and a presidential plane used by John F. Kennedy and Lyndon B. Johnson.

The presidential plane is the only one that's open to the public by guided tour, but you can walk among these moth-balled airplanes to your heart's content.

Other exhibits highlight experimental aircraft and the achievements of NASA, Arizonans who were prominent in aviation, black aviators, women aviators, and the men who flew in B-24 bombers in WW II.

There is an admission charge. Hours: 9 A.M. to 5 P.M. daily, except on Christmas Day. Take I-10 east to the Valencia exit, then go 1.5 miles east to the entrance. For information, telephone (520) 574-0462.

The Titan Missile Silo Museum south of Tucson recalls the drama of the Cold War and provides a close-up look at the machinery of the Nuclear Age with tours of the deactivated nuclear missile silo. Soviet satellites still monitor the site to verify the missile is nonfunctional.
PATRICK FISCHER

TITAN MISSILE MUSEUM

The Titan Missile Silo Museum south of Tucson in Green Valley is a satellite facility of the Pima Air & Space Museum. It's the only museum in the world displaying a relic of the Cold War era, a deactivated intercontinental ballistic missile, the Titan II.

When the Titan II site was being readied as a museum, the missile itself was moved above ground so Soviet Union satellite-imaging devices could verify that the warhead had been removed. As additional proof of peaceful intentions, the 740-ton launch door was welded into a half-open position.

Tours of the Titan Missile Museum include a video presentation of a missile launch and an underground look at the silo, which floats on massive springs in order for the silo and missile to withstand a direct hit from a bomb or missile.

Countdown procedures, security features, and monitoring programs are explained by the guides, and visitors see the 740-ton door that blocked the entrance to the launch-control room.

An admission fee is charged. Hours: November through April, 9 A.M. to 5 P.M. daily; May through October, 9 A.M. to 5 P.M., Wednesday through Sunday.

Reservations are recommended. Take I-19 south from Tucson to Exit 69 (Duval Mine Road); turn west to the museum entrance. For information, telephone (520) 625-7736.

WHIPPLE OBSERVATORY

Clear skies, absence of light pollution, and minimal air turbulence make for a very active astronomy industry in southeast Arizona. Observatories top some of its highest peaks.

One of these is the Fred Lawrence Whipple Observatory atop Mount Hopkins in the Santa Rita range, 36 miles south of Tucson. Jointly built and operated by the Smithsonian Institution and the University of Arizona, the 4,744-acre site includes the innovative Multiple-Mirror Telescope.

The Whipple visitors center, which includes a picnic area, is 10 miles east of I-19 in the foothills of the Santa Rita Mountains. Because the road to the observatory is narrow and winding, a locked gate prevents visitors from driving to the mountaintop. However, bus tours are available by reservation.

To drive to the visitors center from Tucson, leave I-19 at Exit 56 (Canoa Road). Take the east frontage road three miles south to Elephant Head Road. Drive east 1.6 miles to Mount Hopkins Road. Turn south and go 5.5 miles to the parking area.

Tours are available March through November on Mondays, Wednesdays, and Fridays. Reservations are required up to four weeks in advance.

For information about tours, contact Whipple Observatory, P.O. Box 97, Amado, Arizona 85645. Telephone (520) 670-5707. ◩

WHEN YOU GO

The drive to **Colossal Cave Mountain Park** southeast of Tucson takes nearly a half hour from the central part of the city, and the guided tour there runs about 45 minutes. There's also an adjacent county park with a picnic area and campground.

It will take you at least half a day to tour **Biosphere 2**. There's a restaurant, gift shop, and a hotel at the site. Allow about 45 minutes to drive there from downtown Tucson.

A "must-see" attraction for anyone who visits Tucson, the **Arizona-Sonora Desert Museum** takes at least half a day to wander through. Most of the exhibits are outside, so bring a hat and sunscreen. A restaurant and a gift shop are on the premises.

Old Tucson Studios will entertain almost anyone for two hours or more. You'll find several restaurants and a saloon. It takes about a half hour to drive from downtown Tucson.

You can spend a couple of hours or all day exploring either the west or the east unit of **Saguaro National Park**, depending on the activities that you choose to do. You can tour the visitors center, go for a drive, or hike. There is water at the visitors center, but bring lunch and carry water if you go for a hike in the desert.

Allow at least an hour and a half to reach the **Kitt Peak Observatory.** Once there, you'll need a couple of hours to take a tour and explore the visitors center, which provides a wealth of information on the observatories and astronomy.

There are rest rooms, water, and pop machines but no food, so bring your own and enjoy the lovely picnic areas complete with tables and grills. The gift shop features astronomical and Tohono O'odham Indian items. A donation of $2 is suggested. Telephone (520) 318-8726 for hours and tour times.

An hour or more should allow you to soak up the ambiance at **Mission San Xavier del Bac**. Allow another hour if you plan to attend Mass. A gift shop is at the mission and native food and crafts are available in the cooler seasons.

Pima Air & Space Museum can take all day if you are a dedicated airplane aficionado. There's a snack bar and large gift shop at the museum. Telephone (520) 574-0462.

Titan Missile Silo Museum is about a half-hour drive from Tucson. Guided tours last one hour. Telephone (520) 625-7736 for reservations. Walking shoes are a must; high heels are prohibited. ♇

In a mere 26 miles, the winding Mount Lemmon Highway climbs nearly 7,000 feet in elevation through spectacular scenery, ranging from the desert floor at Tucson to the tall pines atop the mountain.
INGE MARTIN

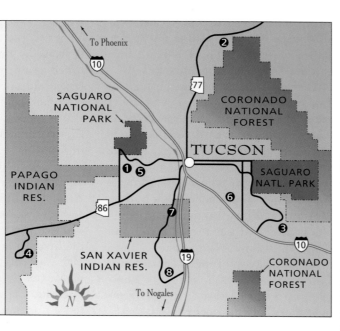

❶ Arizona-Sonora Desert Museum

❷ Biosphere 2

❸ Colossal Cave

❹ Kitt Peak Observatories

❺ Old Tucson

❻ Pima Air Museum

❼ San Xavier del Bac Mission

❽ Titan Missile Museum

SOUTH TO
OLD MEXICO

Chapter 3

Every time I pass the turnoff to Mission San Xavier del Bac, going south out of Tucson toward Nogales on Interstate 19, I feel that I'm driving backward in time over one of the oldest roadways in the Southwest. Native

people traded along the Rio Santa Cruz, which the roadway follows, for millennia before the Spanish missionary Padre Eusebio Francisco Kino first entered Arizona via this route in 1691.

Passing Tubac, the first permanent European community in Arizona, I recall that Captain Juan Bautista de Anza, commandant of the presidio there, led a party north along the Santa Cruz to the Gila River, and then west into California. The route that he blazed is now a national historic trail.

A lot of history has been laid down along this road between Tucson and Nogales. Just reciting place names along the way — Tubac, Tumacácori, Calabasas, Guevavi, Ruby — summons up a storied past of Indians, conquistadors, and missionaries.

Many settlements in Arizona can claim great age, Tubac among them. There were already Europeans in Arizona by the time Tubac was established as a frontier fort in 1752, and villages had sprung up around mission churches built by Jesuit missionaries. But it's fair to say that Tubac was the first permanent European community in Arizona.

In 1752, life along the frontier in what the Spanish called the Pimería Alta, the upper lands of the Pima Indians, was tumultuous. In the previous year the Pimas had rebelled against the Spanish presence, killing more than 100. Carrying out orders of the viceroy of Mexico to protect Spanish colonial interests, Captain Tomás de Beldarráin led a contingent of 50 troops to the

(OPPOSITE PAGE)
Missionaries established the first Spanish settlements in the Southwest beginning in 1691 when Father Eusebio Francisco Kino scouted a location for the Guevavi Mission in the Santa Cruz River Valley, near where the partially restored Tumacácori Mission now stands.
RANDY A. PRENTICE
(ABOVE) *Grasslands near Sonoita are suited for cattle.*
DAVID ELMS, JR.

44

de Anza entered California at the confluence of the Gila and Colorado rivers and made his way north to found the city of San Francisco. Today, de Anza's path is a national historic trail.

The history of Tubac is a pattern of decline and revival, all tied in with shifting allegiances in Europe and the protection of mission churches and nearby villages against Apache maraudings. Thus in 1775, when authorities in Mexico City ordered the presidio moved north to Tucson, the little settlement of Tubac was left defenseless.

The village revived in 1787 when another garrison was established there. But by the time the Gadsden Purchase had brought southern Arizona and other parts of the Southwest into the United States in 1853, Tubac was virtually a ghost town. Fortune smiled again, however. With the discovery in the 1860s of rich silver lodes nearby, Tubac became for a while the largest town in Arizona.

The *Weekly Arizonian*, the territory's first newspaper, was published in Tubac, one of the few villages anywhere, certainly, that can claim ghost town to boom town status in less than 10 years.

Nowadays Tubac is a boom town of another sort. Just off I-19, 45 miles south of Tucson, the village touts itself as the place where "art and history meet." The history part is mostly taken care of at the Tubac Presidio State Historic Park, the first-established of Arizona's state parks, where artifacts of presidio days and remnants of the original fort itself are preserved in the park museum. The park also shelters a school erected here in 1860.

With more than 80 shops, galleries, and studios, Tubac has become an art community. The Tubac Festival of Art is just one of several special events. An annual art walk takes visitors into working studios and galleries, Anza Days celebrate the explorations of Captain de Anza, and throughout the year the Tubac Center for the Arts sponsors several exhibits and events.

TUMACACORI

Walk just south of Tubac Presidio State Park to the picnic grounds across the road and you will find a very old footpath. Now officially a

(ABOVE) The remains of Spanish soldiers and settlers rest in the campo santo at Tubac Presidio State Historic Park. Established in 1752, the walled fort of Tubac Presidio helped protect settlers from Indians. DAVID W. LAZAROFF *(BELOW) Spanish and, later, Anglo miners dug gold and silver ore from the hills surrounding Tubac, then ground the ore with a simple animal-powered mill called an arrastra.* EDWARD McCAIN

Indian village of Tubac, three miles north of Mission Tumacácori. There, on the west bank of the Santa Cruz River, Captain Beldarráin ordered the foundations laid for the Presidio San Ignacio de Tubac. By 1757, the walled fort and the settlement that grew around it sheltered more than 400 persons.

In 1774, Captain Juan Bautista de Anza, who had become presidio commandant in 1759, blazed a route from northern Sonora into California across the scorching desert of southwestern Arizona. He named the route el Camino del Diablo, "the devil's highway." Two years later, via a more northerly path,

national historic trail running from Nogales, Arizona, to San Francisco, California, it's the route forged by Captain Juan Bautista de Anza back in the 1770s. From the Tubac Presidio you can crisscross the Santa Cruz River for 4.5 miles on the Anza Trail south to Mission Tumacácori, which, along with two other very old structures — Guevavi and Calabasas — comprise the Tumacácori National Historical Park.

In 1701 Guevavi was the first *cabecera*, or main mission church, established in Arizona by Padre Eusebio Francisco Kino. Kino's idea was that riding out from Los Santos Angeles de Guevavi, a priest could serve mission outposts called *visitas* in Sonoita, Calabasas, and Tumacácori.

When Carlos III of Spain ordered that Jesuit fathers be expelled from the Pimería Alta in the summer of 1767, the churches were abandoned until Franciscan missionaries replaced the Jesuits a year later. The Franciscans assigned to Guevavi relocated mission headquarters to the broad Santa Cruz Valley at Tumacácori. Neglected, Guevavi began to crumble. Today, only three eroded low walls remain of Guevavi, the oldest surviving Spanish Colonial Jesuit structure in North America.

Until his retirement a few years back, my friend, Nick Bleser, spent part of every day at the Mission San José de Tumacácori. Nick's passion is history in general, the history of the Pimería Alta in particular. He would agree, I'm sure,

The soft glow of luminarias (paper bags with sand and a candle) light the interior of Tumacácori Mission on Christmas Eve.
EDWARD MCCAIN

with the judgment of another history buff, author William Faulkner, who declared, "The past is not dead. It's not even the past."

"When you walk into one of these old places," Nick says, "you enter the last day of its existence as an active site, and you have no idea what happened before that moment." Nick's job as an interpretive specialist with the National Park Service at Tumacácori was to find out what went on at Tumacácori, Guevavi, and Calabasas and to pass along some of his knowledge to visitors.

The ruin at Calabasas, on high ground above the Santa Cruz River, is enclosed by a chain-link fence topped by concertina wire, razor sharp. The ground inside the enclosure is littered with broken glass, beer cans, even some sardine tins from back in Civil War days. A corrugated-tin roof on a steel frame protects the ruin from wind and rain. But the effects of erosion have been hastened by the work of vandals and fortune hunters who undercut the foundations with their digging. There's not much left to look at.

But these weathered walls, encompassing a rich past, are a historian's dream, according to Nick Bleser. "It's got everything," he says. "It was a visita of both Guevavi and Tumacácori. It became a rancho. Gándara, provisional governor of Sonora, tried to buy it and make it his headquarters. There's the Mexican Period and the Civil War when it was the commanding officer's headquarters for Camp Moore just across the wash . . . there's mining . . . the first land scheme . . . the Apaches . . . the railroad."

Nick Bleser campaigned hard for the protection of Calabasas and Guevavi. With the creation of Tumacácori National Historical Park in 1990, what remains of these two venerable places will be better served.

At present, neither site is open to the public. Eventually, the park service hopes to build a visitors center at

The day's first light illuminates the Pimería Alta Historical Society Museum in Nogales, Arizona. The building was the community's original city hall.
Arthur Patrick Mullin

Calabasas from which it could then carry van loads of tourists to Guevavi.

Tumacácori National Historical Park is 48 miles south of Tucson on I-19, at Exit 29. The park is open daily, 8 A.M. to 5 P.M. It is closed on Thanksgiving and Christmas.

NOGALES

Citizens down here like to refer to the cities along the international line between Mexico and Arizona as Ambos Nogales, which means "both Nogaleses." They are twin cities — not quite separate, not quite one.

Wide paved streets, fast-food franchises, discount department stores, auto parts chains, and supermarkets on the Arizona side; cobbled side lanes, curio stores, pottery shops, *helado* (ice cream) vendors, and *abarrotes* (small grocery stores) in Sonora.

Nominally, two languages are spoken — Spanish among citizens of Sonora, English among Arizonans — but what you hear mostly are the lilting cadences of Sonoran Spanish on either side of the line. Many shopkeepers and clerks in Ambos Nogales are bilingual, shifting between two languages with admirable ease. For commerce, the lingua franca is often "Spanglish," one of those innovative combinations that arise when two cultures and two languages collide, and then merge.

The annual *Cinco de Mayo* (fifth of May) celebration commemorates Mexico's victory over French invaders at Puebla, Mexico, in 1862. The celebration includes a parade that starts at Nogales High School in Arizona and moves south toward the border. There are floats, dancers in costume, school kids carrying banners. The mayor and other important persons stand in open cars and wave to pedestrians. As the last few floats ease away from the staging area, the high school band breaks into a spirited, broken-tempo version of *On Wisconsin*. A bit odd for the Cinco de Mayo fiesta, I'm thinking, but a good marching tune nonetheless.

Next to the holiday celebrating Mexico's independence from Spain on September 16, 1821, Cinco de Mayo is the biggest festival, and the streets approaching the border are lined with

MADERA CANYON

I'd wager that at least half of the committed bird-watchers in the United States have targeted southeastern Arizona for a bird-watching junket. The region is a bird-watcher's paradise because it harbors more species than almost any other area of comparable size in the United States.

Accounting for these great numbers of birds are the "sky islands," the high, heavily forested mountains that contain isolated wet canyons. One such wet canyon is Madera Canyon in the Santa Rita Mountains south of Tucson and east of Green Valley.

With birds migrating through the sky islands, encounters with the unexpected are routine for birders in Madera Canyon. The broad-billed hummingbird, sulphur-bellied flycatcher, elegant trogon, and flammulated owl are among the rare birds that have been spotted in the canyon. Two hundred thirty species of birds have been counted in Madera Canyon and more than 100 species of birds are known to breed there.

Prime birding season in Madera Canyon is March through September. Then, birders flock to the Santa Rita Lodge Nature Resort, located beside a stream in the heart of the canyon, at an elevation of 4,800 feet.

At the beginning of the season there are waves of migrating birds. Then permanent residents move in to nest. Later, in July and August, when the summer monsoon rains inspire flowers to bloom a second time, hummingbirds — as many as 14 species of them — begin to feed voraciously. For other birds the arrival of the monsoons is like a second spring, a second mating and breeding season.

However, my favorite time to observe nature is winter, which, of course, is mild in southeastern Arizona. I may not see as many kinds of birds, but even in winter a birder can expect the unexpected. One December while hiking near Madera Canyon I saw an Aztec thrush and a rufous-backed robin, both strays from Mexico. Occasional Mexican strays scoped by birders in Madera Canyon and other sky islands include the gray silky-flycatcher, golden-winged warbler, yellow grosbeak, varied thrush, and the berylline hummingbird.

Birds, of course, are not the only wildlife story at Madera Canyon. The Santa Rita Mountains are prime habitat for black bears, mountain lions, deer, fox, coyotes, bobcats, rare insects, and a variety of snakes.

Once while hiking in a remote canyon, I spooked a young black bear. I was startled. The bear was scared out of its wits. It fled in such frenzied haste that it appeared that its rump would bowl over its ears.

To reach Madera Canyon take I-19 south from Tucson to the Continental Road exit at Green Valley. Turn east and follow the signs 12 miles into the canyon. The gradual ascent makes for an easy drive.

Many bird-watchers book reservations at the Santa Rita Lodge a full year in advance. For information, telephone (520) 625-8746.

Autumn sycamore leaves decorate the bird-watchers' haven of Madera Canyon in the Santa Rita Mountains south of Tucson.
DAVID MUENCH

(ABOVE) *Twin arches mark the border crossing between the two Nogaleses where throngs from the United States and Mexico cross daily to buy goods.*
JACK DYKINGA
(ABOVE, RIGHT) *Brightly costumed children join in the Cinco de Mayo parade along Grand Avenue in Nogales, Arizona.*
(OPPOSITE PAGE) *Celebrants crowd Avenida Obregón for the annual Cinco de Mayo parade from Nogales, Arizona, to Nogales, Sonora.*
BOTH BY EDWARD McCAIN

celebrants. At the border, Mexican customs officers salute and wave the marchers, floats, and autos through the gate and into Mexico.

Quickly I walk the few blocks from the crossing to Avenida Obregón, the main parade route through Nogales, Sonora. I make my way to the corner of Calle Aguirre and Avenida Obregón, marveling at what I see. The street is festooned with banners and down the avenue, as far as I can see, Obregón is lined with people, standing three and four deep, waiting for the start. Everyone in town, it seems, has come out for the parade. Little kids perch on their fathers' shoulders. People lean out of windows or stand on balconies overlooking the street. Vendors selling ice cream, soft drinks, cotton candy, dolls, and balloons hawk their wares.

That half of the city's population not watching the parade is in it, judging from the look of it. Hundreds of school kids in uniform, girls in pinafores and boys in white shirts and dark pants, horse around, impatient for the parade to begin. At the head of each group a few of the bigger kids carry banners announcing their academic affiliation: "Escuela Emiliano Zapata," one reads. There are firemen in full gear riding in cherry-red fire trucks and police cadets in smart new uniforms, ready to march. There are marching bands, drum and bugle corps, rifle teams, mariachi groups. There are charros on horseback wearing broad-brimmed, black-velvet sombreros trimmed in silver. And almost every float or automobile hood is adorned by a beautiful dark-haired girl in sparkling costume, elaborately coiffured and made up.

It's 10 A.M. and already the sun is hot. But hardly anyone shows the least sign of impatience an hour after the scheduled start time, not even the beauty queens in their layered costumes.

The mood remains light, festive. Then suddenly, far down the street near the head of the line, there's a muffled flourish of trumpets. The school kids jump back into place; the cadets snap to attention. And the parade moves slowly away.

Tucked in between a contingent of volunteer firemen and a group of grade-school kids, I spot a car-dealer's float from the Arizona side. I wave. Those on the float wave back, and someone shouts, "¡Arriba! Ambos Nogales — two cities, one heart, one fiesta."

Maquiladora plants, sometimes called "twin plants," are American-owned factories in Mexico. There, Mexican workers assemble seat belts, kites, electronic coils, garage-door openers, computer components, apparel, wood frames, Velcro hooks and loops, microphones, stuffed animals, and countless other products. They are assembled from parts shipped from the United States. The finished goods are returned to the United States for sale and distribution.

Maquiladora derives from the Spanish *maquila,* meaning a percentage of grain or ground flour paid by farmers to the miller as a grinding fee. Thus, a foreign-owned assembly plant in Mexico is required by law to return a percentage of its profits, a maquila, to its Mexican employees.

At the Nogales port of entry, fruits and vegetables make up the greatest volume of commercial traffic between Mexico and the United States. In fact, more fruits and vegetables are trucked across the border here than at any other international crossing in the world. Annually, several million tons of produce enter the United States at Nogales for shipment throughout North America and to Europe and Japan. More than half the fresh produce sold in Canadian and American supermarkets in winter is grown in Mexico and shipped through Nogales, to the tune of some $40 million in customs duties.

Nogales was founded in 1880 by a pioneering merchant, Jacob Isaacson, who set up a trading post at Nogales Pass. The city's name comes from the many *nogales,* "walnut trees" lining the canyon through the pass. In 1899 the Territorial Legislature decreed a new county, Santa Cruz, and made Nogales its seat of government.

The original Santa Cruz County Courthouse, neo-classical in design and constructed of stone quarried in the area, was erected in 1903. The courthouse was named to the National Register of Historic Places in 1978.

Dwarfed by its neighbors, Pima County to the north and Cochise County to the east, Santa Cruz is the smallest county in Arizona, but it occupies an area larger than the entire state of Rhode Island. Wide-open space is one thing there's plenty of in southeastern Arizona.

SHOPPING IN NOGALES

Most American shoppers in Nogales, Sonora, are tourists on their first trip to Mexico. They roam Avenida Obregón, soaking up the sights and sounds of old Mexico. Usually they want to purchase an inexpensive souvenir at one of the curio shops to take back to the home folks. Most find what they come for: serapes, tequila, a Seri Indian carving, a sampling of Mexican coffee, leather goods, a photo of themselves sitting astride a burro and wearing a sombrero, hand-blown glasses, an onyx chess set .... and the list goes on. They will have heard that Mexican shopkeepers are aggressive in their sales tactics, that prices are inflated, and that you have to be prepared to haggle over price.

Vendors *are* aggressive and they say a lot of things, some of them funny, to get you into their shops. Once, as I was walking in front of a leather goods store, the owner called out, "Belt, señor? Looks like you need one." Caught off guard, I looked down at my belt. It was an old favorite of mine, faded and cracked, and I always wore it with faded blue jeans. But he was right; it sure had seen its better days. I smiled. "Okay, let's see what you've got," I said, and walked inside and bought a belt. The seller assured me the belt was hand-tooled. I

BACK ROAD TRIP
FROM WETLANDS TO GHOST TOWN

(BELOW) *Montana Peak towers above Ruby.*
(BOTTOM) *This rusty slide once was shiny from use by squealing children.*
BOTH BY JOHN DREW

For a back road trip that includes some beautiful country, a wetlands wildlife refuge, a peek at a well-preserved ghost town, a hike into a scenic canyon, and winds up at a jewel of a lake, take the road to Ruby and beyond.

From Tucson, drive south toward Nogales and the Mexican border on Interstate 19. (I-19 is the only highway in Arizona signed in kilometers; multiply by .6 to get equivalent in miles.) About 41 miles south of Tucson, leave the highway at Exit 48, Arivaca Junction. Pick up Arivaca Road, angling southwest 20 miles to Arivaca. Your back road adventure begins here, gradually at first because the road all the way to Arivaca is paved, easy going, passing through rolling grassland, prime cattle country.

On the outskirts of the village of Arivaca, population 150, give or take a country cousin or two, you pass a parking area on the left where a sign marks the entrance to the Arivaca Cienega, a wetland portion of the 114,000-acre Buenos Aires National Wildlife Refuge. Park here and pluck a map from a covered rack at the entrance. The map and other printed materials locate hiking trails within the refuge and provide information on wildlife. Depending on the time of the year, if you hike across the cienega or along Arivaca Creek on the other side of town, you might catch a glimpse of migrating waterfowl and shore birds.

To visit the main portion of the sprawling Buenos Aires National Wildlife Refuge, drive 12 miles west on Arivaca Road, then south on Sasabe Road to the entrance. The refuge was created in 1985 to preserve habitat for the endangered masked bobwhite quail. White-tailed deer and mule deer roam its extensive acres. Pronghorns, reintroduced from Chihuahua, are on the preserve, as well as more than 237 bird species that have been identified there. Checklists of birds and mammals may be obtained at refuge headquarters.

The truly back road segment of this side trip starts on Ruby Road, looping some 35 miles southeast from Arivaca to I-19, gravel most of the way. Along the way, Ruby Road rises steeply into the Atascosa Mountains, winding past the ghost mining town of Ruby, through the Pajarita Wilderness at Sycamore Canyon, and on past Thumb Rock and Peña Blanca Lake to the interstate.

Ruby's owners allow hiking, picnicking, and bass fishing with the purchase of a permit, or you can peek at Ruby, southern Arizona's best-preserved ghost town, from the locked gate on Ruby Road. If you've brought along a pair of binoculars, you can even zoom in on some of the buildings. For information, telephone (520) 744-4471, or write Ruby Mines, 6202 West Ina Road, Tucson, Arizona 85743.

Another way to get a closer view of the town is to keep your eye out for another airing on your home-town station of *The Ghosts of Ruby*, a program about the natural history of the abandoned mining town, presented by the PBS television series "Nature." For

today, though, a peek from the gate will have to suffice.

At Sycamore Canyon in the Pajarita Wilderness five miles east of Ruby, a short trail takes you from the parking area down to Hank and Yank Springs. Well-known muleskinners and U.S. Army scouts, Henry "Hank" Hewitt and John "Yank" Bartlett ranched here in the 1880s. In 1886 the ranch was attacked by Apache marauders. Yank was wounded and a neighbor, Phil Shanahan, was killed. Johnny Bartlett, Yank's 10-year-old son, escaped and ran to Oro Blanco, nine miles away, to summon help.

All that remains of the ranch are a few crumbling walls near the spring and a sign that recalls Hank and Yank's battle with the Indians, which is a lot more than can be said for most people, on both sides, who died during the Apache Wars.

You can hike in Sycamore Canyon downstream to the Mexican border. It's a 12-mile round trip, but you don't have to go that far to appreciate the beauty of this sweet little wilderness canyon and the variety of its flora and fauna. Of course, if you want to see the big stands of spreading Arizona sycamores

that give the canyon its name, you will need to lace up your hiking boots and hoof it almost all the way to the end.

The last time I hiked into Sycamore Canyon it was early January. On the road coming across from Arivaca, I had encountered rain, sleet, and a snow squall heavy enough to turn me around temporarily.

In the canyon itself there was a dusting of snow on the leaf litter underfoot and, in the shadiest nooks, a thin pane of ice glazed over quiet pools. It was cold and I'd brought only a light jacket. Hiking out, I remembered a time in mid-July when I'd stripped naked and splashed in a cool, deep pool farther downstream.

Driving out to I-19 from Sycamore Canyon, I recalled earlier trips. We used to park our car near Peña Blanca Lake and ride mountain bikes on the gravel road 10 miles over rolling terrain to Sycamore Canyon.

We had lunch beside the stream, took a short nap, enjoyed a quick dip in cool creek water, and then began the long ride back. At Peña Blanca Lake, Ruby Road merges with the paved State Route 289. From there it is another 10 miles back to I-19. ⮱

(ABOVE, LEFT) *Scenic Sycamore Canyon in the Pajarita Wilderness on the United States -Mexico border cuts its path through stone beneath a canopy of its namesake tree.*
JACK DYKINGA
(ABOVE) *Springtme at Peña Blanca Lake, west of Nogales, means fishing in near-perfect weather, as long as it's catch and release. Peña Blanca and Arivaca lakes are currently restricted due to mercury contamination. Only the trout are mercury-free.*
INGE MARTIN

smiled again. Maybe. In any case, it was a handsome belt.

Did we haggle over price? You bet. But I didn't insult him; nor did I cheapen his wares by offering half of what he asked. You haggle because you know there are no fixed prices, and frequently there are no price tags. So you ask, "How much?" The answer, almost always, is, "I'll make you a special deal." Then the merchant gives you a price.

Trying it on for size, I admired the belt, praising its craftsmanship. Then I offered $3 less than his asking price. "Oh no, señor," the shopkeeper countered. "I cannot give you the belt." I started to slide it off. "Maybe I could give you one dollar off," he said quickly.

Eventually, we agreed to split the difference. He beamed from ear to ear and I walked away happy, not only with the belt but with the encounter. He was a good salesman; I liked him. It's a good belt; I still wear it with blue jeans.

Many shops are filled with curios, souvenirs, and trinkets. But many others specialize in high-quality goods and you can find excellent furniture, pottery, stoneware, glassware, silver crafts, and clothing.

Brilliantly colored paper flowers are among the myriad crafts and curios sold on the streets and in the shops in Nogales, Mexico. Shopping across the border almost always guarantees bargains on leather goods, furniture, and silver.
DAVID BURCKHALTER

TRAVELING IN MEXICO

Visas and Insurance: U.S. citizens visiting Nogales, Sonora, for less than 72 hours do not need a visa. However, if you stay longer or travel 25 kilometers beyond the border, you'll need a tourist card, which is free with proof of citizenship and photo identification. If driving in Mexico, you'll need a vehicle permit and Mexican auto insurance. Check with a travel agent for details.

Duties: Re-entering the United States, you must declare all items bought in Mexico. The first $400 of goods per person (that includes children) is exempt. The next $1,000 worth of goods is subject to a 10 percent duty. If you have more than $1,400 in goods, the amount of duty depends on the items and the intended use.

Information: You may call the Mexican Consulate General in Nogales (Arizona), (520) 287-2521, or in Phoenix, (602) 242-7398. Two Internet sources are the home page of Mexico's Ministry of Tourism (http://mexico-travel.com) and the consular information sheets available from the U.S. State Department (http://travel.state.gov).

Cautions:
- Always carry proof of your citizenship: a passport, original naturalization papers, certified birth certificate, or a notarized affidavit.
- Always carry proof of automobile ownership and proof of insurance that's valid in Mexico.
- Do not carry weapons or ammunition of any kind into Mexico.
- Avoid purchasing prescription drugs in Mexico. U.S. Customs may ask that you produce a physician's prescription.
- To avoid the risk of having your pet quarantined for several weeks upon your return to the U.S., check with U.S. Customs before taking your animal into Mexico.

PIMERIA ALTA MUSEUM

The Pimería Alta Historical Society Museum occupies the old Nogales, Arizona, City Hall on Grand Avenue. Dedicated in 1915, it's an elegant old building, designed by Henry O. Jaastad, the architect who also designed St. Augustine Cathedral in Tucson. The Pimería Alta is a region where cultures have met and mixed for 10,000 years. The museum interprets and preserves that history.

One small exhibit, "Medicine on the Frontier," featured items that doctors carried in their black bags back then, various surgical instruments, and patent medicines.

Not surprisingly, many of the surgical tools were used to extract bullets or arrowheads. One bullet probe is a slender, flexible rod with an unglazed porcelain tip. If the physician, while probing, struck a lead bullet, the porcelain tip was marked with dark streaks. The next step was to use one of the specialized forceps to extract the bullet.

The museum also houses a small collection of historical works about Pimería Alta, publishes articles about the region in its monthly newsletter, and offers a number of museum-sponsored trips to its members and others. Many

Rancho de la Osa
GUEST RANCH

His name is Fred. He's long-legged in boots and blue jeans, smiles his white-toothed smile from beneath a ten-gallon hat, and seems to be everywhere . At dinner he stands behind the serving table, wrapped in a white chef's apron and holding aloft an oversized ladle. "Come on up and let me give you some more of this here barbecue, George," he sings out. Fred makes a point of remembering the name of each ranch guest.

After dinner we walk over to the cantina, and there's Fred behind the bar. Mesquite logs blaze in the big fireplace; a big-screen television lights up the opposite wall.

Sunday morning at breakfast, Fred's passing around a sheet on which he's asked guests to write their names and state their horse-riding ability. After breakfast we all head to the stables and there's Fred wearing chaps and a battered hat. Gone is his grinning, hospitality-host face. Now, he's got on his serious head-wrangler's face. That's Fred's real job, you see, to make sure that each of the paying guests at Rancho de la Osa, smack against the Arizona-Mexico border fence in the foothills of the Baboquivari Mountains near Sasabe, gets safely mounted — and stays mounted — for daily rides.

The ranch dates to pre-territorial days. Its name derives from a long-ago incident when a black bear cub wandered onto the hacienda one day. Cute, the cowboys thought, and began to play with the cub. Suddenly, a full-grown female bear, frantically searching for her lost cub, charged into the courtyard. The cowboys managed to rope her, but it took all afternoon to wrestle the bear into submission and drag her off the premises. Rancho de la Osa means "ranch of the she-bear."

My mount is named Puro, "cigar" in Spanish, picked for his age and gentleness since I'd signed up as a horseriding beginner. It's either late winter or early spring — you can't always be too sure in southeast Arizona. At 9 A.M. we're all bundled against the chill, but by mid-morning we've shed our jackets.

We ride at an easy pace into nearby hills over classic Sonoran Desert terrain and make a long loop back to the ranch, covering some 15 miles, according to Fred. Back at the ranch, we change into swimming suits and head to the heated spa for a long, hot soak before Sunday dinner — prime rib with all the trimmings and home-baked pies for dessert.

For information on Arizona guest ranches, contact the Arizona Dude Ranch Association, P.O. Box 603, Cortaro, Arizona 85652, or visit their web site (www.azdra.com). You may call Rancho de la Osa at (520) 823-4257 or (800) 872-6240. ◪

(LEFT) *A cowboy hat might be more stylish, but a helmet is safer, especially for the inexperienced rider.* (BELOW) *Riders at Rancho de la Osa guest ranch hit the trail through the grasslands along the border near Sasabe.*
BOTH BY EDWARD MCCAIN

of these trips are into Mexico's interior.

The Pimería Alta Museum in Nogales is located at the corner of Grand Avenue and Crawford Street. Telephone (520) 287-4621.

PATAGONIA AND BEYOND

Given Patagonia's currently placid appearance, you'd never guess that right up until the onset of World War II, it was a town in which you might want to avoid main street on a Saturday night — unless you were itching for a fight. The nearby hills and canyons were salted with mining camps. On Saturday nights hard-rock miners would wash the grime from their necks and ears, and spill out of their camps in places like Mowry, Flux Canyon, Harshaw, Duquesne, and Washington Camp, and mix it up with the rough-and-tumble cowboys in Patagonia.

At a Patagonia cafe I once met a man, then in his 80s, who had been town constable back then. "It got pretty rough sometimes," he said matter-of-factly. "I never shot anyone, but I did have to pistol-whip a man once. He came at me with a knife."

That's all gone now. The mines are worked out, the miners dead or gone, and, although one or two saloons might get a bit raucous on a Saturday night, knife fights and bar brawls are pretty much a thing of the past.

Patagonia has gone to the birds. It might be fair to say, in fact, that birds, bird-watching, and wildlife generally helped revive the local economy.

The birds were always here, of course, finding excellent breeding and nesting habitat in the Santa Rita and Patagonia Mountains, along Sonoita Creek, and in the San Rafael Valley and Canelo Hills east of the valley. But what makes the region especially great for bird-watchers are a couple of wildlife sanctuaries managed by The Nature Conservancy.

One of them, the Patagonia-Sonoita Creek Sanctuary, a 320-acre riparian strip running right through town, is

(LEFT) *The white flower of the sacred datura blooms in southern Arizona's San Rafael Valley, an area with some of the finest cattle country in the West.*
BRUCE GRIFFIN
(ABOVE) *An abandoned miner's cabin stands in Duquesne, just one of the boom-to-bust mining towns on southeastern Arizona's ghost town trail.*
RANDY A. PRENTICE

57

home to more than 200 species of birds. The other is Canelo Hills Sanctuary, approximately 20 miles south of Sonoita on State Route 83. So popular has birding become that on a spring weekend at the Sonoita Creek Sanctuary in Patagonia, you're likely to run into bird enthusiasts from almost anywhere in the world.

As a less than hard-core birder myself — although I love birds — what mostly brings me to the Patagonia area are its natural beauty and its opportunities for outdoor recreation, mountain biking especially.

Pedaling a mountain bike, I've toured many of the old mining camps in the Patagonia Mountains. Almost all of them are ghost towns now, although a few die-hards still hang on at Washington Camp. Weekends, my mate and I would head into the hills from Patagonia on Harshaw Canyon Road (Forest Road 49) to the ruined town site of Mowry, 13 miles south of Patagonia, where we would set up our camp for the weekend.

From Mowry, we ranged all over the Patagonia Mountains and down into the San Rafael Valley. One Saturday we rode across the valley, where the headwaters of the Santa Cruz River bubble to the surface, on to the Canelo Hills and up to Canelo Pass, where we picnicked in the shade of piñon pines.

Below us lay a wide sea of emerald-green grass broken by the darker canopy of foliage where the Santa Cruz channel bisected the valley.

Another day took us halfway across the valley, south through the vast acreage of the San Rafael Ranch, and on to Lochiel, smack against the Arizona-Mexico border. After lunch we pushed north along the central ridge of the Patagonia Mountains and back to Mowry, a loop of some 30 miles, we figured. We arrived at camp tired, hungry, elated — and saddle sore.

The next day we broke camp, loaded our bikes, and drove across the San Rafael Valley, through Canelo Pass, then north approximately 15 miles to the village of Elgin, the hub of southeastern Arizona's wine industry.

Travelers happening upon this wine district usually are amazed. Wine grapes, I suppose, are not often associated with southern Arizona. But viticulturists in Appellation Sonoita, as the district is officially known, discovered that locally abundant sunshine, good red soils, cool nights, and dependable seasonal rains provide ideal conditions for growing wine grapes.

After lunch in Elgin, we headed west four miles on Upper Elgin Road to State Route 83 and Sonoita. There we gassed up before driving a few miles north to the road leading into the rolling, oak-flecked grassland hills of the Empire/Cienega Resource Conservation Area, a 45,000-acre preserve administered by the U.S. Bureau of Land Management.

Situated in a high desert basin between the Whetstone and the Santa Rita mountains, the preserve supports one of the few true grasslands remaining in the state. In some parts of the range grasses grow to six feet.

Cienega Creek, from which the preserve derives half its name, rises to the surface near the original Empire Ranch headquarters. We camped along Cienega Creek beneath a canopy of Frémont cottonwoods, some of the largest I've seen anywhere in Arizona.

The next day we would cycle up a steep trail into Mattie Canyon in the Whetstone Mountains. The ride would test our ability to handle mountain bikes over really rough terrain. ⚘

(BELOW) *Green grapes will ripen and hang heavy on the vine at harvest time in Arizona's wine country near Sonoita.*
EDWARD McCAIN
(BOTTOM) *Cienega Creek flows among the cottonwoods and willows of the the Empire/Cienega Ranch, a Bureau of Land Management preserve north of Sonoita.*
JERRY SIEVE

WHEN YOU GO

The bird-watching mecca of **Madera Canyon**, about an hour from downtown Tucson, is a great place to spend an hour enjoying a picnic, all-day hiking, or several days if you overnight at the campgrounds or the lodge.

Tubac Presidio State Historic Park, an hour from town, will take an hour or so to explore, while the mission at **Tumacácori National Historical Park,** just 4.5 miles down the road, will take another hour. You'll probably want to take another hour or two to wander the art galleries and shops, and have lunch at one of the restaurants of the growing art colony of Tubac.

Driving the back road to **Arivaca** and **Ruby** will take the better part of a day if you stop and smell the cactus blossoms along the way. You can get a bite to eat at Arivaca, but all services are closed at **Peña Blanca Lake**. Be sure to take a dependable car, and in case of emergency, always carry drinking water and food and tell someone where you're going and when you plan to return. If the weather is wet, don't go.

Buenos Aires National Wildlife Refuge is about an hour's drive from Tucson, and you'll want to take at least a couple of hours to explore the

preserve. Pack a lunch, as there are no restaurants nearby.

Nogales' **Pimería Alta Museum** will take about two hours to tour. A number of restaurants are nearby.

The San Rafael Valley communities of **Patagonia, Sonoita,** and **Elgin** are about an hour from Tucson or a half-hour from Nogales. You'll want to spend the day taking in the scenery, exploring the ghost towns, quaint communities, and bird sanctuaries. There are restaurants in or near each of the communities. 〽

Looking north at the Sasabe border crossing on State Route 286, the bulk of Baboquivari Peak rises in Arizona. The sign cautions drivers in Spanish to watch for pedestrians.
EDWARD McCAIN

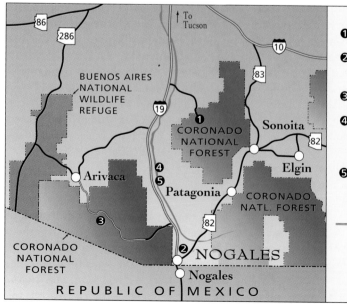

❶ Madera Canyon

❷ Pimería Alta Museum

❸ Ruby

❹ Tubac Presidio State Historic Park

❺ Tumacácori National Historic Park

— unpaved road

HERITAGE OF
THE OLD WEST

COWBOYS, CAVALRY,
AND MINERS —
THEIR LEGACY LINGERS
ON THE LAND

Chapter 4

Every fall since 1952, the community of Willcox down in southeastern Arizona's Cochise County has celebrated Rex Allen Days in honor of a native son who became the last of the silver screen's singing cowboys. At the Rex

(OPPOSITE PAGE)
The restored Cochise County Courthouse now serves as the centerpiece of Tombstone Courthouse State Historic Park. It is filled with memorabilia and interpretive displays from the region's Wild West days. RICHARD MAACK
(ABOVE) *Grave markers still stand on Tombstone's Boot Hill.* EDWARD MCCAIN

Allen Museum, movie posters trumpet: "Starring Rex Allen, the Arizona cowboy, and KoKo the miracle horse." The posters are for films such as *Old Oregon Trail, Utah Wagon Trail, Under Mexicali Stars, Arizona Cowboy, Phantom Stallion, Thunder in God's Country, Last Musketeer,* and *Old Oklahoma Plains* — all showcasing Allen's considerable singing talents. Allen's recording of *Streets of Laredo,* for example, sold more than 3 million copies.

A bronze statue of Allen stands in a city park across from the Rex Allen Museum; and KoKo, who lived for 27 years, is buried there.

Dancing in the streets, riding, roping — all are part of the festival atmosphere of Rex Allen Days. Proceeds go to charity.

America's love affair with the Old West made Rex Allen a star, and it keeps tourists coming to Cochise County year after year to visit Old Fort Bowie, the Geronimo Surrender Site in Skeleton Canyon, the Cochise Stronghold, the O.K. Corral in Tombstone, and such other remnants of the Old West as the Copper Queen Mine in Bisbee, the Gadsden Hotel in Douglas, rancher John Slaughter's house, and Fort Huachuca, home of the famed Buffalo Soldiers.

TOMBSTONE

If Wyatt Earp had not lived in Tombstone, "The Town Too Tough to Die," its citizens would have needed to invent him. In a manner of speaking, they did. Earp — tall, lean, and clean-featured — rode to the town's rescue,

The boardwalks, hitching posts, and false-front buildings of Tombstone's Allen Street preserve the ambiance of the 1880s, when the town boomed, and the Earps and the Clantons strode its dusty streets.
RICHARD MAACK

but not in the standard Western horse-opera sense. You know the stereotyped scenario: rough-bearded, armed outlaws hold a community hostage until the good guys in white hats ride in on their palominos and run the bad guys off.

The playbill for Tombstone's legendary Western drama lists a cast of characters who include Wyatt Earp and his brothers Morgan and Virgil; card-sharp Doc Holliday and his girlfriend, Big Nose Kate; the Clanton gang; and a pair of outlaws named Johnny Ringo and Curly Bill. The stage sets are familiar: the Crystal Palace Saloon, O.K.

Corral, and Boothill Cemetery. The denouement is a gunfight at the O.K. Corral, of course, where a half-minute fusillade of gunfire kills three of the Clanton gang. On the other side, Virgil and Morgan Earp and Doc Holliday, a dentist in real life, are slightly wounded.

In the aftermath, Morgan and Virgil Earp are ambushed; Morgan is killed, Virgil crippled for life. A vengeful Wyatt Earp tracks down and kills three men he holds responsible for the attack on his brothers.

The gunfight at the O.K. Corral did happen, no question. But in the telling and retelling — by word of mouth, in

books, on television, in the movies — the details have been played with fast and loose. And only in the most oblique way do they have anything to do with the legend of "The Town Too Tough to Die."

With blond hair and piercing blue eyes, Wyatt Earp fit the physical image of the quintessential Western lawman. But although he had been a lawman in Dodge City, Kansas, Wyatt Earp never was Tombstone's town marshal. That position was held by Virgil Earp, who was also a deputy federal marshal. Sometimes, when things got rough, Virgil deputized one or more of his brothers. Two other Earp brothers, James and Warren, arrived in Tombstone with the rest of the clan in 1879, but did not participate in the famous gunfight.

At the time, Tombstone, scarcely a year old, was a mining boom town. Soldiers from Fort Huachuca had taunted the town's founder, grizzled prospector Ed Schieffelin, for combing the barren hills surrounding the San Pedro River Valley. "All you'll find out there is your own tombstone," they teased. Schieffelin eventually filed four mining claims. Perhaps with a twinkle in his eye, he named the first two Graveyard and Tombstone.

When the Earp brothers arrived, Tombstone may still have been a sorry little mining camp of a few hundred hard-rock miners camped around a central saloon. But Wyatt Earp, who earned a living by gambling and investing, speculatively, in mines, saw great potential for profit. Perhaps he also had a talent for prophecy. Within a year of Earp's arrival, the town had swelled to nearly 15,000, the largest population in the entire territory.

By then Tombstone had become the most important "metropolis" between El Paso and San Francisco. Thick-carpeted hotels, their fine dining rooms decorated with oil paintings, offered menus printed in French and fine food and wines served by white-jacketed waiters. Big operators from the East got wind of the wealth of the Tombstone silver strike and were soon on the scene, striking deals over drinks served across mahogany bars in long-stemmed crystal glasses. There were masked balls with ladies in expensive gowns, theater, elegant weddings, chamber music, and seafood iced and delivered from California by stage — all that an urbane society could wish for.

It ended almost as suddenly as it had begun. When water started to infiltrate mine tunnels, the owners installed pumps to siphon off more than 6 million gallons daily — but it was futile. One mine after another closed. Some reopened, briefly, but by 1910 Tombstone was headed toward oblivion, right along with Charleston, Millville, Fairbank, and other satellite communities it had spawned. By 1929, Tombstone had declined so far that the

(LEFT) History buffs can tour the well-preserved Bird Cage Theatre, where top vaudeville acts once played.
(BELOW) Editor John Clum, who founded the Tombstone Epitaph May 1, 1880, gave the newspaper its name because "every tombstone has its epitaph." The Epitaph is still publishing more than a century later.
BOTH BY RICHARD MAACK

county seat was moved south to Bisbee. Coincidentally, Wyatt Earp died that year in California.

Exactly what transpired to put nine men with firearms face to face in a vacant lot behind the O.K. Corral on October 26, 1881, is still open to supposition. The Clantons, it is known, were big-time cattle rustlers, a fact which by itself would have put them crosswise with the law, namely Virgil Earp. Wyatt Earp was rumored to be working undercover for Wells Fargo at that time, helping to track down stagecoach highwaymen and bank robbers, but there's no documentation to support such conjecture.

To add to this potboiler plot: Johnny Behan, the rather feckless Cochise County Sheriff, was a friend of the Clantons. He and Wyatt Earp were already political enemies when Behan's mistress, Josephine Marcus, abandoned him to move in with Earp. The animosity between them thickened, to say the least. Regional historians seem to agree that all those things foreshadowed bloody violence.

After the shoot-out, Wyatt Earp did not stick around for long, leaving Tombstone early in 1882. Over the years, he drifted from mining camp to mining camp, gambling or taking odd jobs in law enforcement.

Amid Tombstone's boom and bust, the gunfight at the O.K. Corral, although sensational enough in its lawlessness to cause President Chester A. Arthur to threaten to impose martial law, was insignificant. But when Tombstone's citizens looked around in the 1960s for a way to keep this tough little town alive, they found it down at the O.K. Corral.

The Tombstone Courthouse, the oldest standing territorial courthouse in Arizona, was already a state park and tourist attraction. Clearly, people were interested in the Old West, especially in its wilder, rough, shoot-'em-up manifestations. So "The Town Too Tough to Die" transformed itself into a kind of Western theme park.

U.S. Route 80 going through town was moved closer to Boothill Cemetery, making it a more accessible roadside attraction. The Bird Cage Theater, the Crystal Palace, Nellie Cashman's Boarding House, and Fly's Photography Gallery were spruced up. And several edifices were pinpointed for their historical importance, including the offices of the *Tombstone Epitaph*, established in 1880 ("every Tombstone has its epitaph," said newspaper founder John P. Clum).

Today, Tombstone flourishes because myths about the Wild West die hard. Dozens of businesses there trade on the public's insatiable curiosity about the Old West, real or imagined. Some of Tombstone's citizens roam its boardwalks in old-time Western garb and sit around its saloons looking like characters off a movie set. And the legend that sparks the most avid tourist interest is that of Wyatt Earp and the gunfight at the O.K. Corral.

BISBEE

When I drove through the tunnel at Mule Mountain Pass to catch my first glimpse of Bisbee sprawling helter-skelter along Tombstone Canyon and up the surrounding hillsides, I had a profound sense of having seen it before. I hadn't, of course; I was new to southern Arizona then. On weekends I'd pick a destina-

tion, hop in my pickup, and drive to it. One weekend I chose Bisbee because a novelist friend had told me: "Check out Bisbee. I hear it's a writers and artists colony, sort of."

I remember vividly my first reaction to Bisbee: "This is a mining town!" I shouted. I had not yet seen the enormous open pit beside the road, nor the mine tailings piled high, but it was a mining town — I was sure of it.

Its resemblance to other mining towns I'd known 35 years ago and 2,000 miles northeast in the Upper Peninsula of my home state, Michigan, was uncanny. They had the same small houses, only two or three rooms each. They were built on the same precarious perches, marching in tiers up the steep hillsides. And there was the same mix of building materials — frame, stone, adobe, and corrugated roofing.

So much did Bisbee resemble those Copper Country mining towns that I recalled pasties, a food popular with Michigan miners. I started to look around for a storefront with a sign announcing "Fresh Pasties For Sale." There was none. But not long ago, I asked a Bisbee friend if he knew what a pasty was. "Oh sure," he replied. "It's a small meat pie. The Cornish miners here used to carry them underground in their pockets."

From Tombstone Canyon, Bisbee's main street, countless concrete stairways rise steeply to the tiny houses on narrow lanes on the canyon's sides. One summer weekend I spent two days exploring Bisbee on those dizzying stairways. It was an adventure. Full of excitement, I'd lace up my hiking shoes and begin climbing a steep pitch of what appeared to be at least a hundred steps (some flights have more than 250 steps), following them to where they disappeared amid green foliage.

A mile high, Bisbee's a leafy place and one of the leafiest of green things is ailanthus, the "tree of heaven." It was imported from China. Like kudzu, introduced from Japan into the southern United States, ailanthus has grown thickly anyplace it can get a spot on

(OPPOSITE PAGE) *Tombstone's Crystal Palace, restored to its 1881 glory, still serves thirsty customers in grand style.*
RICHARD MAACK
(ABOVE, LEFT) *A stairway threads its way between buildings on its climb up a precipitous hillside in historic downtown Bisbee.*
GILL C. KENNY
(ABOVE) *Well-built brick buildings make up much of Bisbee's downtown, nestled in Tombstone Canyon in the Mule Mountains near the Mexican border .*
RANDY A. PRENTICE

which to cling — bare ground, cracks in concrete, or between fence slats.

Often the steps ascended to a small landing where they'd jog right or left before continuing upward. Once or twice I dead-ended at someone's garden gate. At one of those gates, I met an elderly woman who took pity on my exertions and offered me a glass of cool lemonade.

That afternoon I discovered the out-of-the-way studio of a jeweler who worked with native turquoise and other regional gemstones.

On the second day, after climbing several nearly vertical stair-ways and breathlessly hiking up a steep street, I came across the Muheim Heritage House Museum. A fine 10-room mansion, it was once the residence of Joseph M. Muheim, an early-day Bisbee entrepreneur.

Bisbee was, of course, a mining town — and what a town it was. Copper was queen. Over nearly 100 years, millions of tons of ore were gouged from the Sacramento and Lavender pits or blasted and hauled from 2,000 miles of under-ground shafts in the Copper Queen and other mines. At the height of its prosperity, around the turn of the century, Bisbee's population was roughly 35,000, the largest in all of Arizona.

Like all mining towns, where men performed dangerous work under dreary conditions for long hours, Bisbee had its wild and woolly side. In Brewery Gulch alone there were more than 50 saloons and perhaps as many "sporting houses." Between San Antonio and San Francisco there was no more splendid a watering hole than Bisbee.

But that splendor dissipated as the mining operations dwindled. By 1940 the population of Bisbee had declined to about 5,000. Even as the famous Lavender Pit opened in 1951, giving impetus to a short-lived economic resurgence, many businesses had already closed and a lot of miners had moved on. Boarded up storefronts, vacant houses, potholed streets, weed-plagued yards — Bisbee took on a woebegone, forsaken appearance.

After years of reduced production,

(ABOVE AND RIGHT)
Whether for lunch on the veranda or a night's stay, the venerable Copper Queen Hotel in the heart of Bisbee's historic district is worth a visit. The 44-room hotel opened in 1902 and added an air of elegance to the mining town, especially to boisterous Brewery Gulch, the street to its immediate right, where miners caroused through 68 saloons and sporting houses.
EDWARD McCAIN
RICHARD MAACK

layoffs, and brief recoveries, the Phelps Dodge Corporation finally shut down operations in Bisbee in December 1974.

But Bisbee hung on. Encouraged by cheap housing and a blessedly moderate year-round climate, artists, craftspeople, and writers migrated to Bisbee. Among them were friends of mine, who in 1983 bought what they affectionately refer to as "our little miner's shack" up a steep hillside just off Tombstone Canyon. Soon, commercial fronts in Tombstone Canyon, Brewery Gulch, and along Subway Street were lined with craft shops, bookstores, painters' studios, jewelers' workshops, art galleries, coffee shops, restaurants, and bed-and-breakfast inns. Some lasted, some didn't. Each time I came over from Tucson, a shop or restaurant had gone out of business and another had sprung up in its place.

A local poet organized the Bisbee Poetry Festival; others brought in a bicycle race, La Vuelta de Bisbee, a five-day stage race. Since the race has gone on hiatus at times, check with the Bisbee Chamber of Commerce for status and dates. And the racing spirit lives on. Recently, after many years of absence, kids racing self-designed coasters speed down the mile-and-a-half length of Tombstone Canyon on Fourth of July weekend. In October there's the Bisbee

1,000, also billed as "The Great Stair Climb" because the course climbs the many flights of concrete steps, exactly 1,034, on Bisbee's hillsides. It's "the 5K that feels like a 10K," race posters advertise, and, having spent the better part of two days clambering up and down those stairs, I can personally vouch for that.

The start-finish line for the Bisbee 1,000 is the front stairway of the Cochise County Courthouse, a splendid pueblo-deco style structure built in 1931 after the county seat was moved from Tombstone to Bisbee. Below the courthouse stands a large iron statue of a heavily muscled man wielding a hammer. Called *Iron Man*, it's a tribute to the hard-rock miners.

Although the mines are shut down, it's the aura of mining that attracts many visitors to Bisbee. They are not disappointed. Men who worked in the mines lead the underground tours of the Copper Queen Mine and surface tours of Lavender Pit and the Historic District.

The Bisbee Mining and Historical Museum, located in the shadow of the famous Copper Queen Hotel, occupies the 1895 General Offices of the Phelps Dodge Corporation. The museum interprets Bisbee's mining and cultural past.

It's Saturday morning and I'm standing against the fence at the Lavender Pit

A number of entertaining events hosted by Bisbee's residents attracts visitors from all over the region to the picturesque town. (BELOW, LEFT) *Roger Bristow charges up 157 stairs while carrying an eight-pound block of ice in the Barco Iceman Carry, a side event at the Bisbee 1,000.* ED COMPEAN (BELOW, RIGHT) *The Tombstone Canyon Coaster Race runs through the heart of downtown Bisbee.* MARTY CORDANO

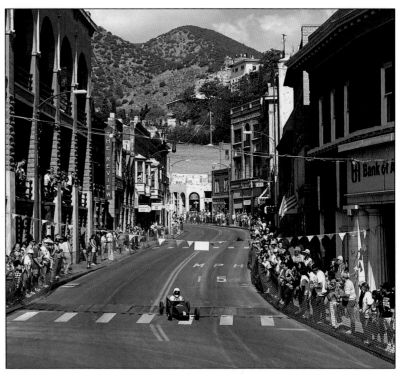

mine, going cross-eyed trying to count the tiers of benches spiraling down to the bottom of the pit. "Hi there," a voice calls cheerily. I look up to see a strapping older man, perhaps in his 70s, stepping smartly toward me.

"What do you think of the pit?" he asks, extending his hand. But instead of a handshake he places a small booklet, about the size of a religious tract, into my hand.

"It's really something, very impressive," I answer warily, steeling myself for the sermon that's sure to come.

"Used to work down there … over there, too, in the underground," he says, waving a meaty palm in the direction of the Copper Queen. "Right where you're standing used to be part of the town of Lowell," he continues. "All the people had to leave when they started on the pit."

We talked, or rather, he talked, I listened. He'd seen it all, it seemed. He'd worked underground, starting when he was in his teens, and later in the big pit. He'd been laid off and called back. As a kid, he'd witnessed big labor troubles that led to the deportation by rail of striking miners in 1917. When the mines closed, a lot of men, including himself, looked for another living. For a

(BELOW, BOTTOM) *Former miners like Neto Chavez guide visitors dressed in slickers, hard hats and miners' lamps through the miles of shafts and stopes at Bisbee's famous Copper Queen Mine.*
TOM TILL
PETER KRESAN

while he had guided tours underground in the Queen Mine, but the work didn't suit him, he said.

It was getting close to noon. "Well, I've got to meet some friends for lunch. Nice meeting you," I said, handing back the pamphlet he'd laid on me when he walked up.

"It's only two dollars," he said. Surprised, I looked closely at the tiny booklet. *Souvenir of Bisbee by a Re-cycled Miner* was its title. "That's me," he said pointing at the name, Ray Ewing, on the cover. "It's about Bisbee and me."

"What a sales job," I thought. Until the last I hadn't realized anything was for sale. I bought two copies, one for a friend. It was about Bisbee and Ray Ewing, about all the things we'd been talking about and more. From miner to author of chapbooks. That's a piece of recycling, all right, a major piece.

MINE TOURS

I was wearing a wool sweater beneath a heavy yellow slicker provided by the tour guide, yet I was cold. We'd been in the mine only 30 minutes. It was time enough, though, for the chill and dampness of the constant 47 degrees Fahrenheit winter and summer, to seep into my bones. I thought about the schoolchildren who used to flee to the mines for safety when they were warned of an Apache raid. Scared kids, shivering with fear and cold, waiting for the town siren to sound the all-clear. We rode into the tunnel on the same skinny little train cars that used to carry miners to work. Our guide, himself a former miner, told us about the ore-hauling mules that never left the mine. All their lives they lived and worked underground, never seeing the light of day. Some were as blind as bats, he said. A few days later, I took the van tour of the Lavender Pit, the yawning open-pit mine, and the historic downtown district of Bisbee. Both tours are offered daily by Copper Queen Mine and Surface Tours, telephone (866) 432-2071.

DOUGLAS

Wendy Glenn and her husband, Warner, live on the Malpai Ranch several miles out on Geronimo Trail

(LEFT AND ABOVE) *Gleaming marble pillars and the grand staircase define the opulent lobby of the Hotel Gadsden. The hotel opened in downtown Douglas in 1907, burned in 1928, and reopened in 1929. For the better part of the century the five-story landmark has been home away from home for businessmen and dignitaries along the border.*
RICHARD MAACK
JACK DYKINGA

Road, east of Douglas. With the help of daughter, Kelly, who lives on another ranch across the San Bernardino Valley, they run a herd of Hereford cows, Brahma bulls, and some crossbred cattle, about 250 head in a good year when there's been plenty of rain to green up the rangeland. It's hard work — a full-time job, and then some. But it's their way of life. "Warner's family has always been in ranching, and I married Warner," offers Wendy, in simple explanation.

It happens sometimes that the Glenns will dress up, planning to head into town for dinner, but on the way out they see a sick horse or cow down in the corral. "You don't even think about it," Wendy says. "You turn right around, go back up and change to your work clothes and nurse that animal, all night, if you have to."

So there's not much time away from the ranch. But on occasion Wendy manages a shopping excursion into Tucson, where she's invariably amused when store clerks pick up her credit card issued by a Douglas bank and ask,

"Where in the world is Douglas?" Wendy laughs. "I guess we are kind of out of the way down here in this lonely corner," she says.

Tucked up against the borders of New Mexico on the east and Old Mexico to the south, Douglas wasn't always so little-known. It was founded in 1901 as a copper smelter site to process ores brought over from Bisbee. The smelter ran day and night, and Douglas was an important cog in the giant copper-producing machine called the Phelps Dodge Corporation that dominated southeast Arizona's economy for more than half a century. Up on Avenue G, Douglas' main street, the Phelps Dodge Mercantile was a bustling place, while next door at the Gadsden, mining executives, businessmen, ranchers, and cattle buyers from both sides of the border mingled in the hotel's magnificent lobby with its sweeping white marble staircase, four solid marble columns with capitals overlain in 14-karat gold leaf, and vaulted stained-glass skylights.

The story of Douglas' decline is a

"Texas" John Slaughter's ranch house at the San Bernardino National Historic Landmark east of Douglas preserves the ranching lifestyle on the Mexican border of more than a century ago.
JACK DYKINGA

"It's the tallest building in town, a landmark. Everyone knows where it is."

Northeast of Douglas, the vast San Bernardino Valley, Chiricahua Mountains flanking one side, the Peloncillo Mountains the other, runs for some 50 miles before it runs out of room and spills over into New Mexico. It's wild, spread-out country, and life on the cattle ranches is a lot of hard work and loneliness.

Until the late 19th century, ranching was also a desperately unsafe business. Apache warriors still plundered livestock in guerrilla-style hit-and-run raids. That ended with Geronimo's final surrender to General Nelson A. Miles on September 4, 1886, in Skeleton Canyon near Apache, about half way up the valley. It got easier after that, but only a little. Many of these remote ranches, the Glenn family's among them, had to generate their own electricity until a few years ago.

The Glenn ranch and several others in the valley were once part of the much larger spread owned by John Slaughter, a former Texas Ranger who established the 65,000-acre San Bernardino Ranch in the late 1800s. Slaughter, a leather-tough, cigar-puffing 5 feet 6 inches, also served two terms as sheriff of Cochise County when the county seat was still in Tombstone. For his toughness and harsh treatment of lawbreakers he was legendary. It's been said that Slaughter put outlaws on public notice that they should "get out of Cochise County or get killed." Most left.

Now a National Historic Landmark, the ranch house and other buildings sit on approximately 130 acres right on the international border, some 17 miles east of Douglas on the Geronimo Trail. An adjacent 2,300-acre portion of the ranch was purchased by the U.S. Fish and Wildlife Service and has become the San Bernardino National Wildlife Refuge, consisting of natural springs, wetlands, ponds, and grassland. The refuge protects habitat for a variety of wildlife, including 216 species of birds, rare amphibians, and two endangered fish, the Yaqui topminnow and the Yaqui chub.

To reach the Slaughter Ranch, drive east from Douglas on 15th Street, which becomes Geronimo Trail Road.

familiar one. Like a lot of southeastern Arizona towns, Douglas hitched its fortunes to a single industry — mining. When the ores petered out, the industry collapsed. Although the smelter kept on operating for a number of years, it finally had to shut down, too. Douglas fell on hard times. Today, the town is trying to reinvent itself, becoming a kind of service center for Mexican maquiladora plant workers who come across the border to shop in Douglas supermarkets, chain stores, and fast-food franchises.

The Gadsden Hotel, in all its somewhat faded splendor, is still there, of course, and its lobby is still a favorite meeting place for travelers from as far away as Mexico City or Guadalajara. "It's been here since territorial days," says hotel manager, Robin Brekhus.

The entrance to the ranch is 17 miles east of Douglas. Visiting hours are from 10 A.M. to 3 P.M. Wednesday through Sunday. For more information, telephone (520)558-2474.

The San Bernardino National Wildlife Refuge is open to the public without charge but by reservation only. Telephone (520) 364-2104.

RAMSEY CANYON

One of several preserves in Arizona owned by The Nature Conservancy, this 280-acre holding in cool, wet Ramsey Canyon in the Huachuca Mountains is another southeastern Arizona bird-watcher's paradise.

During the spring and summer more than 14 different species of humming-birds have been spotted.

The canyon is also habitat for the lemon lily, known in fewer than 20 places in the world, and rare leopard frogs that croak underwater.

The parking area at Ramsey Canyon is limited to 13 spaces. Once filled, no more visitors are allowed. A parking space may be reserved by calling (520) 378-2785.

To reach Ramsey Canyon, drive six miles south of Sierra Vista on State Route 90. The parking area is four miles west of the turnoff.

FORT HUACHUCA

Red Garland played piano in the post band at Fort Huachuca. William "Red" Garland was a journeyman pianist, I guess you could say, who played with many jazz giants, including Coleman Hawkins, Charlie Parker, and Miles Davis. Garland was a favorite of mine.

One April morning in 1984 I came across his obituary in the newspaper. During World War II, I read, Garland had been stationed with the Army at Fort Huachuca. "That's where I really learned how to play the piano," he had said about his time at the base. While there, he had been privileged to play with some of the best jazz musicians in the United States, he said.

I'd driven through Sierra Vista and past the main gate of Fort Huachuca many times, but always on my way to somewhere else. Learning that Red Garland had played at the fort sparked a new interest for me.

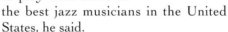

(ABOVE) *Victorian-style homes on Fort Huachuca's Officers Row are among the base's oldest buildings, dating from the 1880s. A one-day home tour, complete with tales of resident ghosts, opens these houses to the public each December.*
EDWARD McCAIN
(LEFT) *The Nature Conservancy preserve in Ramsey Canyon attracts thousands of bird-watchers each year to the east side of the Huachuca Mountains. Today known for its wealth of bird life, Ramsey Canyon a century ago teemed with miners in search of mineral wealth.*
RANDY A. PRENTICE

I knew that until 1947 the U.S. military services were racially segregated. But I did not know that Fort Huachuca had been the main training ground for black fighting units going back to 1898, and that only black units were stationed at the fort from just before World War I to just after World War II.

The first black cavalrymen who were brought to Arizona were mostly former slaves. They were brought to Arizona to fight in the Apache Wars. The Indians called these black cavalrymen "Buffalo Soldiers." Not only were they dark-visaged and curly-headed, but they also possessed the fierce fighting temperament of the buffalo.

Established in 1877 during the Apache Wars, Fort Huachuca is the sole remaining active base of the approximately 70 cavalry posts established in Arizona in the 19th century. Its history is summed up at the Fort Huachuca Historical Museum. The fort is a national historic landmark, and a lot of its nearly 120-year history is exhibited at the museum.

When General John J. Pershing mounted an expedition into Mexico in 1916, he was joined by the 10th Cavalry, one of the units composed of Buffalo Soldiers. During World War I, the Buffalo Soldiers defended the Arizona-Mexico border against infiltration by bandits and saboteurs.

During World War II, when troop strength at the base reached 30,000, black infantrymen were trained at Fort Huachuca. At the end of the war the fort was transferred to the State of Arizona to be used for National Guard training and as a game preserve, but when the United States entered the war in Korea, the fort was reactivated.

In April 1994 in a special ceremony at Fort Huachuca, the U.S. Postal Service unveiled a commemorative stamp in honor of the Buffalo Soldiers.

Unwanted then wanted, that's the checkered history of Fort Huachuca. But throughout, the fort seems to have

(LEFT) *A mountaintop view of the borderlands from the Coronado National Memorial. Coronado may have passed near here on his explorations that took him as far north as Kansas in 1540.*
DAVID MUENCH
(ABOVE) *Fort Huachuca's B Troop commemorates the hard-riding cavalry men the U.S. Army originally stationed at the fort in 1877.*
EDWARD MCCAIN

The moon rises over the Huachuca Mountains and Fort Huachuca's historic Army barracks, constructed in 1883. The fort, built near the end of the Indian Wars, protected the borderlands during the Mexican Revolution. The installation now serves as an electronics and intelligence center for the Army.
EDWARD MCCAIN

been saved by its location. First, it was strategic to the fight against Geronimo. In the early 1900s the fort was ideally situated for guarding the border against possible invaders. Finally, its remoteness, absence of electronic interference, and relatively free airspace made it ideal for its present mission: the Army's Information Systems Command and the home of the U.S. Army Intelligence Center and School.

The Fort Huachuca Historical Museum is open from 9 A.M. to 4 P.M. weekdays, 1 P.M. to 4 P.M. weekends. Closed holidays. For more information telephone (520) 533-5736.

KARTCHNER CAVERNS

In southeastern Arizona, while the tumult of the Apache Wars unfolded above, a silent, eerie world grew from water droplets in a limitless pool of darkness — the hidden, surreal world of an underground cavern.

Now you can see this world, one unexplored by humans until 1974: Kartchner Caverns State Park, nine miles south of Benson off State Route 90, on the east flank of the Whetstone Mountains. Although discovered in

1974, Kartchner Caverns was closed to the public until 1999, so that park planners could be sure visitations wouldn't damage its priceless underground environment.

Kartchner is a living cave system, meaning that the fantastic mineral formations are still "growing" from water slowly seeping through ages-old limestone. Before entering the cave, we tour the park's Discovery Center for background information, then board a shuttle to Kartchner's hillside entrance.

We walk through a series of airlocked chambers designed to protect the cave's delicate balance of steady temperature — 68° F — and almost 100 percent humidity. The last airlock opens into a large high-ceilinged cavern, dimly lit to reveal folds of caramel-colored calcite that appear to flow down the cavern's walls to puddle on the floor. As we stand in awe of varicolored stalactites, hollow "soda straws," twisted helictites, and stalagmites, our guide cautions that touching them will cause irreparable damage.

We descend a ramp to the base of the room and peer across mud flats into the pitch darkness beyond. Soda straw formations glow in the dim light, and paths worn by the cave's discoverers back in 1974 are still visible in the mud.

The tour trail winds among formations that resemble totems and comes to a small alcove that affords us close-ups of a stunning array of mineralized shapes — oxidized striations called cave bacon, draperies of colored stone, and helictites.

Then we step into the Throne Room, an enormous chamber that contains the massive floor-to-ceiling column called Kubla Khan. The grandeur takes my breath away.

The park charges a day-use fee per vehicle into the park. This allows entrance to the Discovery Center, hummingbird garden, picnic areas, and hiking along the six miles of trails. Cave tours are an additional fee. Camping at the park's campground (with either your RV or tent) is a separate nightly fee per camp site. The park is open seven days a week, 7:30 A.M. to 6:00 P.M. For information, call (520) 586-4100. Reservations are a must, sometimes even months in advance. Call (520)586-CAVE (2283) weekdays. ✦

✳
WHEN YOU GO

Historic **Tombstone** is a 90-minute drive from Tucson and you'll want to spend at least half a day traveling back to the days of the Wild West. There are a number of restaurants in town.

Kartchner Caverns, in Benson about one hour from Tucson, requires at least two hours for the cave tour since you must arrive an hour before the scheduled tour. Allow at least an hour for the visitor center's exhibits on the cave, its bat population, and local paleontology. Plan on another hour or two if you want to picnic or hike.

Bisbee, two hours from Tucson, needs a full day just to scratch the surface. Tours of the Copper Queen underground mine, the open pit, and the historic town will use nearly half a day. Seeing the shops, museums, and restaurants may take anotherweekend.

To reach **Slaughter Ranch,** allow at least a half hour to drive the 17 miles east from Douglas on 15th Street, which becomes Geronimo Trail Road. An hour or so will give a good feel for the place.

Drive two hours from Tucson to the town of Sierra Vista and the adjoining **Fort Huachuca.** Bring your vehicle registration, proof of insurance, and driver's license. Allow at least two hours at Fort

Huachuca Historical Museum, (520) 533-5736. Sierra Vista has several restaurants.

For bird-watching in **Ramsey Canyon,** drive six miles south of Sierra Vista on State Route 90 and turn right for four more miles. Stay a few hours or all day. Access is limited, so reservations are highly recommended; (520) 378-2785. Visitors may stay at The Nature Conservancy's Ramsey Canyon Inn, (520) 378-3010. ☛

No letters are mailed from this abandoned post office at the ghost town of Fairbank on the San Pedro River. The town came into existence in 1882 in conjunction with the New Mexico and Arizona Railroad, a short-line rail connecting the Southern Pacific with Nogales.
DAVID W. LAZAROFF

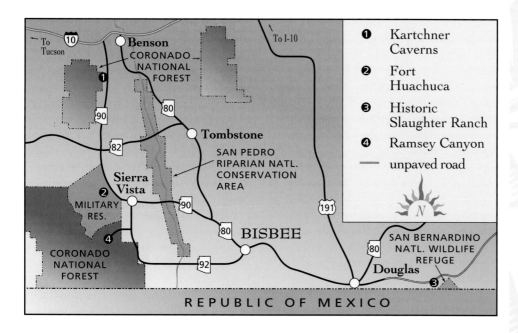

EXPLORING
NATURE'S
SANCTUARIES

Chapter 5

Once while picking my way down a canyon bottom on the west side of the Cochise Stronghold in the Dragoon Mountains, I stumbled upon a place where an otherwise subterranean stream suddenly came to the surface

and flowed for some 200 yards before disappearing again. Enchanted by this dry-land oasis, I scrambled up the side of a large streamside boulder to eat lunch in the shade and listen to the music of water burbling downstream. Atop the boulder I found another surprise — dozens of grinding holes, some worn very deep into the granite, where Apache women long ago ground nuts and seeds into flour. Later, in another place of surpassing natural beauty, I found more grinding holes and on a soaring rock face nearby many pictographs, rock paintings, in which Native American artists had rendered their impressions of the natural and supernatural.

I recall thinking, "Of course, why not in the best places? Places where

water splashes into small pools? Where flowers bloom and hummingbirds flit through sunlight? Where a high rock outcrop looks across a wide valley to a line of trees tracing the bed of a distant river?"

Find a place of great natural beauty in southeastern Arizona and you will almost always find evidence — potsherds, scraping tools, crumbling adobe walls — of the earlier human presence. Whatever their reasons for coming, people have always sought out such places. Today, we acknowledge that impulse by setting aside and preserving settings of special beauty — Willcox Playa, Muleshoe Preserve, Cave Creek Canyon, and others.

But often where people and cultures intersected, conflict arose, and we

(OPPOSITE PAGE) *Amid the oaks of Cochise Stronghold in the Dragoon Mountains, Apache women ground acorns and seeds into meal in bedrock mortars worn into the granitic Council Rocks.* JACK DYKINGA (ABOVE) *Duck Rock is among many stone formations at Chiricahua National Monument.* PETER KRESAN

(ABOVE, RIGHT)
Goldeneye blooms in a grassy meadow in the Chiricahua Mountains' Cave Creek Canyon.
EDWARD McCAIN
(BELOW) *This cozy post office and library serve the small community of Portal and the nearby Southwest Research Station, where naturalists from universities all over the world come to study the canyon's incomparable natural diversity.*
JOHN DREW

likewise memorialize those violent collisions by erecting monuments to their historic importance — Fort Bowie National Historic Site, for example, the field of a bloody battle between Chiricahua Apache warriors and Army soldiers, or the Cochise Stronghold, or Skeleton Canyon, where Geronimo surrendered. Southeast Arizona's landscape is dotted with sites that recall and celebrate both our natural and human history, often at one and the same place.

CAVE CREEK CANYON

I describe Cave Creek Canyon to friends as a mini-Yosemite, so stunning is the beauty of its steep cliffs and rocky pinnacles. From Portal, just a dash from the New Mexico border up at the north end of the San Bernardino Valley, I drive the paved road into the canyon. Driving along at slow speed, taking in the scenery, I glance beyond a roadside fence into a neglected apple orchard. There, perilously balanced, high among limbs sagging with ripe apples, there, to my complete astonishment, is a three-year-old black bear! He reaches for an apple, loses his footing momentarily, grabs the apple and stuffs it whole into his mouth, chewing loudly, juices dripping from his furry snout.

It's the wildlife that brings people to this lovely canyon on the east flank of the Chiricahua Mountains. Birds, reptiles, insects, amphibians, and mammals. University researchers from all over the world come to the Southwestern Research Station, just up the road from here, to study Nature. Amateur naturalists and bird-watchers are drawn to the area in droves. While Portal is in Arizona, the easiest way to get there is to drive two miles north of Rodeo, New Mexico, on U.S. Route 80, then turn west on the paved two-lane for approximately eight miles.

WILLCOX

Willcox, elevation 4,167 feet, founded in 1880. Willcox, a farming and ranching community near the upper end of the long, fertile Sulphur Springs Valley. Willcox, the hometown of Rex Allen, last of the silver-screen cowboys, whose horse, Koko, is buried in a city park. Willcox, a point of departure for trekkers into some of the wildest and most rugged mountains in southeastern Arizona, including the Galiuro, Santa Teresa, Dragoon, Pinaleno, and Chiricahua ranges. Willcox, gateway to Fort Bowie National Historic Site, the Amerind Foundation and Museum, the Cochise Stronghold, and the Chiricahua National Monument.

Willcox is a lot of things to a lot of people, but when I think of Willcox, I think of the playa.

The Willcox Playa, shortened locally to simply the playa (Spanish for beach), is a dry lake bed whose shores touch the south end of town. It's what remains of an ancient lake that geologists call Lake Cochise. It measured 200 miles

around and covered this entire area to a depth of 35 feet. Long ago, woolly mammoths, camels, bison, and giant sloths slogged through the lake's marshes and paleo-Indians camped on its beaches. But when southern Arizona began to dry out around 10,000 years ago, the vast lake's margins gradually diminished. Today, the playa is a 50-square-mile flat, dry lake, so level that its horizontal plane varies no more than a foot over its entire surface.

For years the playa was regarded as a virtual wasteland, good for nothing. During and after World War II the U.S. Army used it for target shooting and bomb testing. Even today, signs warn that the lake bed is seeded with unexploded shells.

Dry as it was, the playa was never really dead, nor was it a wasteland, but few people understood that. After the annual summer rains in July and August, the lake would fill with a couple of inches of water. Suddenly killdeers, sandpipers, avocets, and other shorebirds would appear as if by spontaneous generation. They had come to feed on the several varieties of recently hatched shrimp whose eggs had lain dormant in dried

Broad, sandy, and normally dry, Willcox Playa once held the waters of a vast, prehistoric lake. Each year during the summer wet season it again transforms into a large, shallow lake and teems with freshwater shrimp that attract great flocks of shore birds. In winter the playa is home to sandhill cranes.
JACK DYKINGA

mud for a year or more, waiting for just the right combination of rain and warmth before hatching. The water was ephemeral, of course, but while it lasted, the playa teemed with life.

Water birds of several species — geese, ducks, grebes, herons — historically had come to the playa, and after the bombing stopped they returned. From Canada, Alaska, Montana, Wyoming, and other northern states, sandhill cranes began to return in ever greater numbers to winter at the playa. Now, up to 12,000 of the great, gray birds return to the playa each winter. Roosting by night in several of the playa's shallow ponds, they swarm aloft at dawn to fly to nearby fields to nibble on the grain stubble left over from the harvest.

When people started showing up to observe these birds with their seven-foot wingspans and bugling calls, the townsfolk of Willcox realized they had an important resource in their back yard. The Willcox Chamber of Commerce Visitor Center hands out maps marked with the best places for viewing sandhill cranes on the playa.

In January 1994, the town inaugurated its annual Wings Over Willcox Sandhill Crane Celebration.

MULESHOE PRESERVE

If you're a natural history enthusiast, consider a trip to The Nature Conservancy's 49,000-acre Muleshoe Ranch Preserve 30 miles northwest of Willcox in the Galiuro Mountains foothills. Three-day jeep-hiking trips and four-day horseback excursions are offered four times annually in the spring and fall. TNC personnel accompany the trips and present narrations on the natural and human history of the region.

For information on day visits to Muleshoe Ranch Preserve, telephone (520) 586-7072.

(LEFT) *A mountain meadow crowns Monte Vista Peak, one of Arizona's more spectacular sky islands high in the Chiricahua Mountains.* DAVID MUENCH (ABOVE) *Faraway Ranch was the turn-of-the-century home of the pioneering Erickson family, whose ranch became Chiricahua National Monument.* GEORGE H.H. HUEY

CHIRICAHUA NATIONAL MONUMENT

I'm standing alone atop Sugarloaf Mountain in the Chiricahua National Monument. This is a modest peak by regional standards, only 7,310 feet high, and on a 10-point scale of difficulty it scores maybe a two. It's less than a mile up from where I parked my pickup, but having gained nearly 500 feet of elevation in that short distance, I arrive at the summit puffing somewhat.

The reason I'm alone, though, has nothing to do with the exertion required to get here. It's the weather. It's a raw day in late November. A gusty wind slams against the fire-lookout cabin bolt-anchored to granite, and intermittent dark clouds scud across the summit to spill darts of icy rain.

But between the clouds there's blue sky and sunshine, and from here I can see many of the monument's familiar landmarks. Almost directly below to the south is the famous Heart of Rocks, a fantastic display of weathered spires and balanced rocks with such unusual and well-known rock formations as Totem Pole, Big Balanced Rock, and Punch and Judy. Farther off to the south, I make out the outline of the Turkey Creek Caldera, an extinct volcano that spewed hot volcanic gases over an area of 700 square miles. Below me to the east are Echo Canyon and Massai Point, where trailheads lead into prime hiking country, including Heart of Rocks. And way off north is Cochise Head, shaped like the face of a man reclining — domed forehead, long, curved nose, and a 100-foot pine for an eyelash.

I check the guest register in a metal box atop a steel post before hiking down. People from as far away as Maine, Louisiana, Scotland, and Switzerland have recorded the times and dates of their visits. Some hikers penned their thoughts: "Brrrr ... don't wear shorts" and "Can't write it all on one line" and "Where are the Apaches?"

The entrance to Chiricahua National Monument is 37 miles southeast of Willcox on State Route 186. The monument is open 8 A.M. to 5 P.M. daily, and admission is charged.

The Bonita Campground provides 25 year-round campsites available on a first-come, first-served basis. There is a fee for camping.

Daily tours of Faraway Ranch, a pioneer homestead inside the monument, are offered year-round. Schedules vary with the season. Special events at Faraway Ranch include open house on Christmas and Easter and an ice cream social on Mother's Day.

FORT BOWIE

I found the Apaches over at Fort Bowie National Historic Site. I'd just hiked the 1.5-mile trail into the ruined fort. When I stepped up onto the wide, shaded veranda of the ranger station, which from a distance appears to be a fine old territorial home, I met an Apache family — grandma in long, flowing skirt, mother, dad, a teenage boy in basketball sneakers, two younger girls, and a round-faced toddler with raven hair. They had signed the guest register just before me, and I saw they were from the San Carlos Reservation up near Globe, Arizona. Under comments were two words: "Apache Memories."

The year was 1862. America was at war with itself, north against south, and the troops assigned to the territorial frontier had been moved to New Mexico to protect against incursions from Texas by the Confederate Army. The Chiricahua Apaches moved into the void and once again ruled the region they regarded as their homeland.

On July 15, 1862, a troop of 126 men led by Captain Thomas Roberts was following the route of the Butterfield Stage. The soldiers approached Apache Pass between the Dos Cabezas and Chiricahua mountains on their way from Tucson to New Mexico. Near Apache Springs they

(OPPOSITE PAGE)
Sugarloaf Mountain offers a panoramic view of Chiricahua National Monument's incredible rock formations. Nearly all are comprised of volcanic tuff that has been carved by the elements.
GEORGE H.H. HUEY
(ABOVE, LEFT)
Hikers and campers explore the monument's otherworldly landscapes, such as this slot canyon along the Echo Canyon Trail.
RALPH LEE HOPKINS

were attacked by a force of 700 Indians. The six-to-one odds were overwhelmingly in favor of the Apaches, who had the added advantage of intimacy with the steep, rugged terrain.

But the Army troops, although outmanned, had two howitzers, weapons never before used against the Apaches. Using the howitzers to blast the Apache warriors from their sniper's positions in the rocks, Roberts battled his way through the pass after 10 hours of fighting. It was the biggest battle between the Army and Apaches in Arizona history. Sixty-three Apache warriors were slain. The Army suffered only two casualties.

Twelve days later, Brigadier General James Henry Carleton followed Roberts into New Mexico with 1,400 troops. On his way he stopped long enough to order that a fort be built in Apache Pass. It would be named Fort Bowie and its purpose would be to protect the best water supply available for miles around and to ensure the unmolested passage of wagon trains and stagecoaches.

Fort Bowie survived for 32 years, closing in 1894, some six years after the end of the Indian Wars. A photo taken that year shows an impressive military installation with more than 38 buildings, including a granary, hospital, school, sutler's store, and an elaborate two-story Victorian mansion for the commanding officer.

A few stone foundations and eroded adobe walls are all that remain of Fort Bowie today. Thanks to interpretive materials, including photographs, prepared by the National Park Service, however, visitors can walk among the ruins and in their minds' eyes reconstruct the old fort. To the Apaches looking up at the partially walled fort perched on the high ground above the valley, it must have seemed impregnable.

Walking back to the parking area, I pause beside the spring. I'm alone. Live water spills over rocks beneath a canopy of cottonwood, ash, willow, and walnut trees. It's a beautiful place. I recall the words written in the guest book: "Apache Memories."

To reach Fort Bowie from Willcox,

(ABOVE, RIGHT) *The body of Little Robe, son of Geronimo, is buried in the Fort Bowie cemetery. The two-year-old and his mother were held with other prisoners at the fort when he became ill. He was among three Indian and two white children who died there that summer.*
RICHARD MAACK

take State Route 186 for 22 miles south to a graded road to Apache Pass. Turn east approximately six miles to the parking lot and trailhead. The easy 1.5-mile walk to the fort travels through desert grassland, up through chaparral, and alongside a stream formed by Apache Springs. On the way, hikers can stop at the old Butterfield Stage Station and Fort Bowie Cemetery. The trail is open from sunrise to sunset. Ranger Station hours are 8 A.M. to 5 P.M.

Caution: Although water is available at the fort, hikers should carry a canteen, especially in summer. Avoid hiking during summer thunderstorms when dangerous lightning is present. Be alert for rattlesnakes.

COCHISE STRONGHOLD

In the Dragoon Mountains, about 30 miles across the Sulphur Springs Valley from Apache Pass, lies Stronghold Canyon. It's a formidable place, a natural fortress. Sheer rock walls rise on either side as you enter the canyon and a maze of large granite blocks fools the eye. Cochise, leader of the Chiricahua clan of Apache Indians, fled from Apache Pass into this place in 1860 after he had been falsely accused of kidnapping by a U.S. Army lieutenant recently fledged from West Point and still wet behind the ears.

Cochise knew the Dragoon

PICKING YOUR OWN

Fresh farm produce vended from roadside stands where signs hand-lettered on a scrap of plywood invite you to "pick your own" is probably the last thing you would have thought to put on your agenda of things to see and do in southeastern Arizona. Sure, everybody knows that Arizona's economy was once tied to the five Cs — climate, cotton, copper, cattle, and citrus. And you can, if you want, buy a souvenir jar of prickly pear cactus jelly, mesquite-bean flour, or some such desert vegetable product.

But sweet corn fresh out of the garden? And tomatoes, real tomatoes, the ones that actually taste the way tomatoes used to taste? Black-eyed peas, too, and cucumbers, melons, okra, elephant garlic, lettuce, Concord grapes, peas, beets, cabbage, and, in autumn, squash and Halloween pumpkins?

Yes, indeed. I remember my own astonishment. New to the territory, I was on a weekend excursion, checking out the Willcox Playa and the Sulphur Springs Valley. I had just left Dragoon, a little whistle-stop railroad community butted up against the north terminus of its namesake mountain range. Driving east on Dragoon Road toward the Sulphur Springs Valley, I began to notice trees set down in perfectly even rows, row upon row. Then roadside signs: pecans, peaches, and pistachios for sale. On the next farm there were apples on the bough, red and gold, vast orchards of them.

Reaching the valley, I turned right on U.S. Route 191 and drove south to Sunsites where I stopped at a small cafe for coffee and, of course, apple pie. The waitress greeted me cheerily and asked, "Just visiting?" My Birkenstock sandals and wool socks must have been a tip-off in a room full of men wearing broad-brimmed rancher hats and cowboy boots.

"I am," I said. "By the way, I've been seeing lots of orchards along the road. What do you grow around here?"

"You name it, we grow it," she answered pertly. "Lettuce, pears, beans, peppers, peas ... like I said, 'You name it.'" And she was right. As a matter of fact, I could have said "fish." There's a place north of Willcox off Fort Grant Road that grows catfish and trout. You can catch your own; they even supply the fishing gear.

The place to start is the Willcox Chamber of Commerce and Agriculture. There you can pick up a brochure with a map showing the locations of produce farms and orchards throughout Cochise County and a few in Graham, the next county north. And a harvest calendar shows the approximate time of year when each crop comes to fruition. Some entries are marked "U-Pick Available." If your aim is to carry a basket down through the rows, stooping and picking, you've hit the jackpot.

For information, write to the Willcox Chamber of Commerce and Agriculture, 1500 North Circle I Road, Willcox, Arizona 85643. Telephone (520) 384-2272. For a copy of the brochure, "Fresh Farm Produce," enclose a stamped, self-addressed envelope. ⬩

An apple orchard in the Sulphur Springs Valley, near Willcox, bears a bountiful harvest. Rich soil and plentiful water combine in many of southeastern Arizona's broad valleys to produce a variety of fruits, nuts, and vegetables. At harvest time, visitors can experience the fun of picking the produce themselves for a small fee.
RANDY A. PRENTICE

Mountains well; it is said he was born here around 1814. From 1860 until 1872, Cochise and his band of followers battled the U.S. Army, fleeing into the Stronghold for refuge when necessary. After a negotiated settlement with the Army granting to the Chiricahuas a 55-square-mile reservation in southeast Arizona, their traditional homeland, Cochise lived out his life in peace. He died June 8, 1874, and is buried somewhere in the Stronghold. No one knows where.

To reach Cochise Stronghold from Willcox, travel west on I-10 to U.S. Route 191, Exit 331. Drive south approximately 12 miles to the graded road just before Sunsites and turn west approximately 10 miles into the Stronghold.

The Forest Service operates a campground at the Stronghold on a first-come, first-served basis.

AMERIND FOUNDATION

North of the Dragoon Mountains, not far from where Cochise is buried, there's a cluster of dun-colored Spanish Colonial Revival buildings, each capped with a red tile roof, tucked amid the boulders and oaks of pristine Texas Canyon. This is the Amerind Foundation, a private archaeological research institute whose name, short for "American Indian," defines its purpose.

Founded in 1937 by philanthropist William Shirley Fulton, Amerind's mission is to collect and preserve knowledge, through archaeological research and analysis, of the human cultures that occupied this region. Fulton also believed that studying contemporary Indian cultures could help discover and interpret the past.

Today, in addition to being a widely respected research facility, the Amerind Foundation houses a museum, library, art gallery, and gift shop offering Indian craft arts, books, and photographs. Museum exhibits are varied but include beadwork, masks and shields, costumes, toys, and clothing.

To reach the Amerind from Willcox, travel west on I-10 to Exit 318. Go east one mile to the Amerind turnoff. Museum hours are 10 A.M. to 4 P.M. daily, September through May. Closed holidays. For summer hours and information, call (520) 586-3666. There is an admission charge.

MOUNT GRAHAM

On a crisp sunny day in October, a slight northerly breeze hints of winter as I stand atop Heliograph Peak 22 miles up the Swift Trail (State Route 366) in the Pinaleno Mountains, part of the Coronado National Forest. During the Apache Wars, Heliograph Peak, elevation 10,028 feet, was part of a series of reflective-mirror stations set up by the U.S. Army to pass Morse code messages between military outposts. The military telegraph service, in place since 1873, was largely abandoned during the Indian Wars. Not that it didn't work; when left alone it worked very well. But if summer electrical storms didn't interfere with transmission, the Apaches did, chopping down poles and cutting wires.

On a day like today — cloudless, bright, visibility 100 miles or more in every direction — the heliograph system worked beautifully. From this great height, a Morse code operator, using a device consisting of mirrors and shutters, could redirect the sun's rays in any direction and, with a signal key, flash communiqués to troops in the field or to nearby installations at Fort Grant and Fort Bowie, which were then relayed to distant encampments. During the summer of 1886 alone, more than 800

(BELOW) *Among its many fine exhibits, the Amerind Foundation features a premier collection of prehistoric Mogollon culture pottery from Paquime, Mexico.* (BOTTOM) *Ancient rock writing decorates the granitic rock of Cochise Stronghold in the Dragoon Mountains.*

messages were transmitted throughout the heliograph system, a network of 14 stations in Arizona, 13 in New Mexico, manned and protected by 100 soldiers. After the surrender of Geronimo in September 1886, the system was largely dismantled, but some stations stayed in operation until 1890.

If you could climb the Heliograph Peak Fire Lookout, a padlocked 100-foot steel tower, you would see forever. In all directions, row upon row of mountain ranges are visible from this bird's-eye perch, perhaps the next best thing to flying over southeastern Arizona's basin and range terrain in a light aircraft. Just to the northwest lies the 10,717-foot summit of Mount Graham, the highest point in southeastern Arizona and the fourth highest peak in the entire state.

Surrounded by desert, the broad mountaintop, *dzil nchaa sí án*, "Big Seated Mountain" to the San Carlos Apaches for whom it is sacred, preserves a Pleistocene-relic spruce-fir forest, 14 perennial streams, three high-altitude wet meadows called cienegas, and 18 endemic species of plants and animals. A black bear foraging the mountain may in one day travel

through six distinct life zones. In the spruce-fir forest near the summit, biologists have found bear scat containing seeds from prickly pear fruits consumed in the lower-Sonoran desert scrub down around 3,500 feet.

Cherished by biologists as a type of inland Galapagos, a rare cradle of evolution isolated when glaciers receded 11,000 years ago, Mount Graham is equally prized by University of Arizona astronomers as prime habitat for telescopes. Clear nights with minimal light pollution from nearby cities and towns, low humidity, and no troublesome wind turbulence make the Pinaleno's high peaks ideal for telescope viewing.

Like a lot of other nature lovers, I prize the mountain for its solitude, beauty, and serenity. Tonight, I'll sleep in Treasure Park, a large meadow a couple of miles farther up the road. This late in the year, I'll likely be alone. Last spring when I pitched my tent here, though, I was joined by dozens of campers who had come to see the first bloom of Rocky Mountain irises carpeting the meadow.

Treasure Park's name comes from the rumor that right around the time of

(ABOVE, LEFT) *High atop the Pinaleno Mountains, Hospital Flat, named for an Army hospital established there during the Indian Wars, has offered cool respite to desert dwellers for more than a century.*
WILLARD CLAY
(ABOVE) *The Pinalenos rise more than 7,000 feet from the Gila River Valley to their highest peak, Mount Graham, at 10,717 feet.*
JERRY SIEVE

the 1853 Gadsden Purchase, when Arizona became a United States territory, Mexican outlaws buried 19 pack loads of gold and silver near here. Apocryphal, no doubt, and this lovely meadow's natural beauty is treasure enough for me.

Accounts differ on which of many persons named Graham the highest peak in this crown-jewel mountain range and the county in which it is located got its name. It's hard to say. The best guess, historians seem to agree, is that the honor goes to Lieutenant Colonel James D. Graham of the U.S. Corps of Topographic Engineers.

Safford, the nearby county seat, was named after one territorial governor, so it seems right that one of its recent mayors should have been named after Arizona's first state governor, George Hunt. Affectionately called Gov in his lifetime, Governor Hunt Aker is commemorated at Discovery Park, official visitors center for the Mount Graham International Observatory (MGIO) and a sort of scientific theme park.

At the base of Mount Graham in Safford, before taking a tour up the mountain to the MGIO, visitors may view the Gov Aker Observatory's many exhibits, from life-size displays to hands-on activities. The real excitement starts when you board the Shuttlecraft Polaris, a flight simulator that takes an adrenaline-pumping trek through outer space. On clear nights, you can view the real sky through a 20-inch reflecting telescope. Gov Aker's vision inspired this interactive science museum, which is still under development. Plans include adding a wetlands and wildlife habitat, plus mining, agricultural, and archaeological exhibits. Telephone (520) 428-6260 or visit their Web site (www.discovery park.com).

ARAVAIPA CANYON

Thirty-five miles west of Safford, the Aravaipa Canyon Wilderness, an 11-mile-long canyon with a permanently flowing creek, has been under federal protection since 1969. Large sycamore, ash, willow, and cottonwood trees along the riparian zone provide abundant habitat for birds. Several native fish, primarily minnows and suckers, thrive in the creek. The soft sands along the creek bed reveal the prints of mule deer, black bears, javelinas, coyotes, coatimundis, mountain lions, and other mammals that come to the stream to drink. Lucky canyon visitors sometimes spot bighorn sheep on the canyon's north rim.

Hikers and backpackers may enter Aravaipa Canyon by either the east or west trailhead. Access is carefully controlled by the Bureau of Land Management, however, which issues permits and limits day use in the preserve to 50 persons per day.

For further information on access, permits, camping, and directions to Aravaipa Canyon Wilderness from Phoenix and Tucson, contact the United States Department of Interior, Bureau of Land Management, 711 14th Avenue, Safford, Arizona 85546. Telephone (520) 348-4400.

ROPER LAKE STATE PARK

Recently, after a day of fall bird-watching at Roper Lake State Park and a short hike around the Mariah Mesa Nature Trail, I headed for a soak in the park's hot tub, which is fed by one of many geothermal springs in the area. Three miles south of Safford on U.S. Route 191, Roper Lake State Park is a 240-acre park featuring a 32-acre, spring-fed lake surrounded by cattails and palm trees. Campers, picnickers, swimmers, fishermen, hikers, and bird-watchers are among those attracted to this desert oasis.

The park has 71 campsites available, some with electrical hookups. An island day-use area offers shaded picnic areas and a swimming beach. The Dankworth Pond unit, just a short distance south on U.S. Route 191, is a favorite site for waterfowl and shorebird enthusiasts, but also includes a three-mile hiking trail and a reconstructed Indian Village. Visits to the 10-acre pond and its surrounding 160 acres are limited to day use. Fees are charged for day use and camping. Telephone (520) 428-6760. ▼

Thousands of hikers each year wade through the watery wonderland of Aravaipa Canyon. The designated Bureau of Land Management Wilderness is so popular that a permit system was implemented to limit the number of visitors to 50 a day and preserve the canyon's pristine nature.
MARK S. THALER

WHEN YOU GO

The **Chiricahua Mountains,** about a three-hour drive from Tucson, include **Chiricahua National Monument's** spectacular rock formations, the nearby **Faraway Ranch,** and camping on the west side of the range. On the east side you'll find the beautiful bird-watching area of **Cave Creek Canyon.** There's a general store and cafe in nearby Portal, and Forest Service campgrounds throughout the Chiricahua Mountains. You can spend a day or a week at either of these attractions.

Willcox Playa, to the south of the town of Willcox, is about 90 minutes from Tucson. Allow an hour to several days if the sandhill cranes are there. You can find lodging and restaurants in Willcox.

Fort Bowie is a little more than two hours from Tucson. Allow half a day to explore the old fort and its surroundings. The nearest food is at Willcox.

You'll need at least two hours to tour the **Amerind Foundation,** an hour's drive from Tucson. Be sure to visit the art gallery. The nearest restaurants are in Benson or Willcox.

Cochise Stronghold, about 45 minutes south of the Amerind Foundation, shelters a manicured campground set amid the historic backdrop of the **Dragoon Mountains.** The nearest food is 10 miles east at Sunsites.

Allow at least three hours from Tucson to reach the base of the **Pinaleno Mountains** and another hour to reach their summit, **Mount Graham.** These mountains host numerous campgrounds. Also atop the mountain is 10-acre Riggs Flat Lake, a fine place to fish for rainbow trout. Nearby Safford has hotels, restaurants, and groceries. **Roper Lake State Park** is about five minutes southeast of Safford.

A trip into **Aravaipa Canyon Wilderness** requires a permit from the Bureau of Land Management, 711 14th Avenue, Safford, Arizona 85546. Requests for permits are numerous so apply several months before your trip. Aravaipa is best approached from the west, via an hour's drive from Tucson on State Route 77. Check with the BLM for current road conditions. ♥

Fortunate schoolchildren live the good life amid the pastoral beauty of southeastern Arizona near Dragoon.
RANDY A. PRENTICE

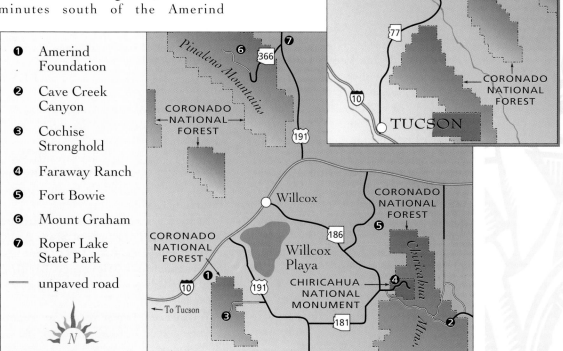

① Amerind Foundation

② Cave Creek Canyon

③ Cochise Stronghold

④ Faraway Ranch

⑤ Fort Bowie

⑥ Mount Graham

⑦ Roper Lake State Park

— unpaved road

Southeastern Arizona hosts many fun and interesting events and activities. Dates vary, so call ahead for exact dates and times, or obtain a schedule from the Metropolitan Tucson Convention & Visitors Bureau, (800) 638-8350 or (520) 624-1817. Performance calendars for Arizona Theatre Company, Tucson Symphony Orchestra, Arizona Opera Company, Ballet Arizona, and other performing arts groups also are available through the visitors bureau.

Telephone numbers are in area code 520 unless otherwise noted.

JANUARY

Tucson Open: Major PGA golf tournament. Fee. 571-0400, www.tucsonopen.pgatour.com.

Wings Over Willcox: Marks return of sandhill cranes to Willcox Playa. Workshops, seminars, bird tours. 384-2272, (800) 200-2272.

Southern Arizona Square & Round Dance Festival: Square and round dancing, clogging. Fee. Tucson. 885-6273, 795-8288

FEBRUARY

La Fiesta de los Vaqueros: Unique to Tucson, Festival of the Cowboys is among the Southwest's oldest rodeos. 741-2233 or (800) 964-5662 or www.tucsonrodeo.com.

Southwest Indian Art Fair: Invitational show and sale by Native American artisans. Food, entertainment, music. Fee. Arizona State Museum, Tucson. 621-6302.

Tucson Gem and Mineral Show: Begun 40 years ago, now the biggest show of its kind in the world. Exhibitors and dealers set up shop in downtown hotels and other sites nearby. 322-5773.

Tubac Arts Festival: One of the longest-running arts and crafts fairs in southern Arizona. Entertainment, food. www.tubacaz.com or 398-2704.

Ruly Amado prepares a pot of "red" at Bisbee's chili cook-off during Brewery Gulch Daze.
TOM TILL

MARCH

Welch's/Circle K Championship: LPGA tournament. 791-5742.

Wa:k Powwow: Tohono O'odham Indian festival at Mission San Xavier del Bac. Inter-tribal dancing, food booths. 294-5727.

Picacho Peak Battle: Reenactment of Arizona's one battle of the Civil War. 1860s demonstrations, fashion show. Fee. 466-3183, (602) 542-4174.

Yaqui Easter Ceremonials: Visitors welcome, but no photographs allowed. Old Pascua Village. 791-4609.

Fourth Avenue Street Fair: Arts, crafts, and entertainment fill downtown Tucson. 624-5004.

APRIL

Tour of the Tucson Mountains: One of Tucson's great perimeter bicycle races. 745-2033 or www.pbaa.com.

Bank One International Mariachi Conference: Mariachis from Mexico and the United States perform. Parade, concerts, folklorico dancing, golf tournament. 884-9920, ext. 243, or www.tucsonmariachi.org.

La Vuelta de Bisbee: Bisbee's three-day cycling event for all ages. 432-5795 or www.azcycling.com.

MAY

Cinco de Mayo: Marks Mexico's 1862 victory over the French. Music, food, dancing. Tucson. 623-8344.

Waila Festival: Celebrates Tohono O'odham social dance music. Demonstrations, O'odham foods. Tucson. 628-5774.

Salute to the Buffalo Soldier: Celebrates achievements of black Army units. Sierra Vista. 459-EVNT (3868).

International Migratory Birding Festival: Bisbee and surrounding areas. 432-5421, (866) 224-7233.

Wyatt Earp Days: Wild-West shootout reenactment. Tombstone. 457-2211, (800) 457-3423.

Patagonia Heritage Festival:
Memorial Day weekend celebration of
Patagonia's past. Entertainment, ice
cream social. (888) 794-0060.

JUNE

Juneteenth Festival: African-
American independence celebration .
Music, food, sports.Tucson. 791-4355.

Sonoita Quarter Horse Show:
Nation's oldest quarter horse show.
Sonoita Fairgrounds. 455-5553.

Balloon Festival: Willcox. Free.
384-3696.

JULY

Fourth of July in Bisbee: Coaster
races, parade, contests, fireworks, food.
Bisbee. 432-5421, (866) 224-7233.

AUGUST

La Fiesta de San Agustín: Outdoor
festival for Tucson's patron saint. 762-
5806, (800) 638-8350.

Southwest Wings Birding Festival:
Field trips, lectures, arts & crafts.
Sierra Vista. 378-0233, 459-3868, or
(800) 946-4777.

Vigilante Days: 10K race, shoot-
outs, hangings, music, chili cook-off.
Tombstone. 457-9317, (888) 457-3929.

**Norteno Music Festival & Street
Fair:** Food, crafts, art exhibit,entertain-
ment. Tucson. 622-2801.

SEPTEMBER

Brewery Gulch Daze: Chili cook-
off, music, food. Labor Day weekend.
Bisbee. 432-5578, (866) 224-7233.

Sonoita Rodeo: Steak fry and dance.
Sonoita Fairgrounds. 455-5553.

Rendezvous of Gunfighters: Pistol
quick-draw artists perform. Tombstone.
Labor Day weekend. 457-2211, (800)
457-3423.

Ft. Huachuca Heritage Days:
Carnival, food, pow-wow, Buffalo
Soldier demonstrations. 533-2374

Oktoberfest: German festival at
Mount Lemmon. Music, dancing, food.
Through mid-October. Fee. 576-1321.

OCTOBER

Bisbee 1000: The Great Stair Climb
5K race up and down the many hills of
Bisbee in mid-October. 432-5421 or
432-7150.

Butterfield Overland Stage Days:
Stagecoach rides, parade, arts and
crafts. Benson. 586-2842, 586-4293.

Anza Days: Celebrates 1775 trek of
Capt. Juan de Anza from Tubac to San
Francisco. Tubac. www.tubacaz.com or
398-2704.

Fiesta De Los Chiles: Everything's
red hot: music, food, and plants. Tucson
Botanical Gardens. 326-9686.

Helldorado Days: 1880s fashion
show, square dancing, barbershop
singing. Third weekend of October.
Tombstone. 398-2704.

Patagonia Fall Festival: Arts and
crafts fair with food, dancing, entertainment. 394-0060, (888) 794-0060.

Rex Allen Days: Willcox honors its
hometown movie-cowboy singing star.
Parade, fair, rodeo. 384-2272 or (800)
200-2272.

NOVEMBER

El Tour de Tucson: One of America's
largest perimeter bike rides. 745-2033.

Festival of Lights: Lighting of
Christmas decorations. Nogales. 287-
3685.

DECEMBER

Christmas Apple Festival: Arts,
crafts, cooking contest, entertainment.
Willcox. 384-2272, (800) 200-2272.

Fiesta Navidad & Festival of Lights:
Christmas caroling and luminarias.
Tubac. www.tubacaz.com or 398-2704.

Luminaria Nights: Tucson Botanical
Gardens. 326-9686.

Territorial Christmas: Antique toys,
ornaments, cards, decorated tree. Sosa-
Carrillo-Frémont House, Tucson. 622-
0956.

Tumacácori Fiesta: First weekend of
December. Traditional crafts, food,
entertainment, Mariachi Mass. Tumacácori National Monument. 398-2341.

Weaving — The Soul of Fiber:
Show and sale of American Indian tex-
tiles and fabrics. Free. Arizona State
Museum, Tucson. 621-6302.

(ABOVE, TOP) *Hot air
balloons ascend among the
saguaros outside Tucson.
Southeastern Arizona fea-
tures several balloon rallies.*
P.K. WEIS
(ABOVE) *The annual
Luminaria Festival lights
the streets of Tubac
each December.*
RANDY A. PRENTICE

INDEX

Mexican revolutionary Pancho Villa straddles his rearing mount in this statue in downtown Tucson. General John J. Pershing led an expedition into Mexico to capture Villa after he had raided Columbus, N.M., in 1916. Pershing did not succeed.
EDWARD McCAIN

PRONUNCIATION GUIDE

acequia—ah-*sec*-kee-ah
Baboquivari—bah-bo-*kee*-vah-ree
bajada—bah-*bah*-dah
Barrio Histórico—*bah*-ree-o ee-*stow*-ree-ko
Barrio El Hoyo—*bah*-ree-o el oy-yo
cabecera—cah-bay-*ser*-ah
Calle Real—*ky*-yay ray-*ahl*
camino—cah-*mee*-no
cienega—see-*eh*-nay-gah
Cinco de Mayo—*seen*-co day *my* oh
Chiricahua—chee-ree-*kah*-wah
Galiuro—golly-*yur*-ro (other pronunci-
   ations abound, including gul-*air*-o,
   gul-*air*-eez, and gul-*lur*-eez)
Guevavi—gway-*vah*-vee
Hohokam—*ho*-ho-kahm
Huachuca—wah-*chew*-kah
mariachi—mah-ree-*ah*-chee
mesquite—mess-*keet*
Nogales—no-*gah*-les
Pasqua Yaqui—*pahs*-kwah *yah*-kee
Picacho—pee-*cah*-cho
Rillito—ree-*yee*-tow
saguaro—sah-*war*-o
San Xavier—sahn hah-vee-*air*
El Tiradito—el tee-rah-*dee*-tow
Tohono O'odham—tow-no *aah*-dahm
Tucson—*too*-sahn
Tucsonenses—too-so-*nen*-says
Tumacácori—too-mah-*cah*-co-ree
vaqueros—vah-*kay*-rows
visita—vee-*see*-tah

(ABOVE, TOP) *The remains
of Camp Rucker still stand
in the Chiricahua
Mountains.*
PATRICK FISCHER
(ABOVE) *The architect of
Tombstone's City Hall
captured the ambiance
of the town's heyday.*
RICHARD MAACK

MAPS

(INSIDE BACK COVER) *Sunset silhouettes the distinctive saguaro cacti of the Sonoran Desert.* CHUCK PLACE (BACK COVER) *The O.K. Corral, site of the gunfight between the Earps and the Clantons, stands as the centerpiece of historic Tombstone.* RICHARD MAACK *Maps were provided courtesy of the Arizona Department of Transportation.*

10 Interstate highway
60 U.S. route
77 State route
═══ Unimproved road
╤═╤ Graded road
▬▬▬ Paved highway
═══ Divided highway
‥‥‥ Historic and scenic road

★ 5.7 ★ Consolidated mileage
✛ Traffic interchange
++++ Railroad
Indian reservation
National forest
Parks and monuments
Urbanized area
Open water

∧ Live stream
⋰ Intermittent stream
⊙ County seat
✈ Municipal airport
500 ft. contour lines
? Tourist information
✕ Roadside rest area
▲ Historic marker

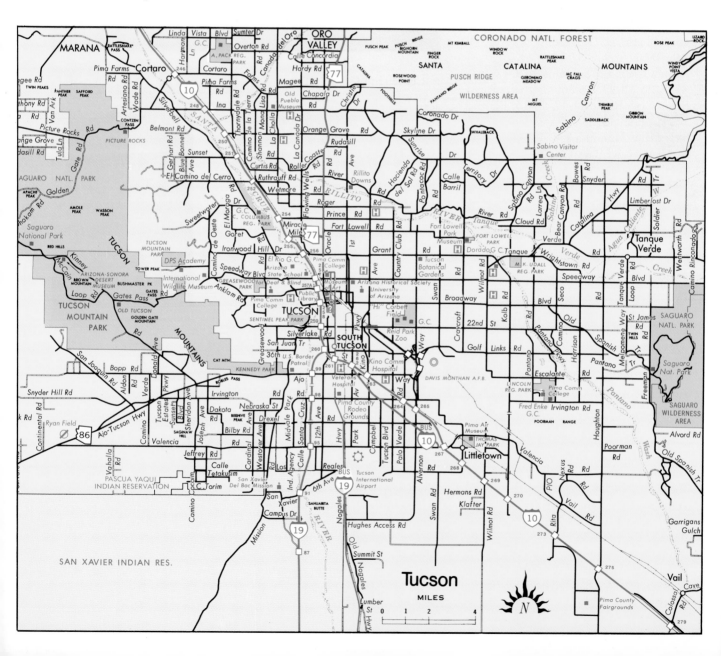

Tucson

MILES

0   1   2   4

N